EVERYTHING IS UNDER CONTROL

EVERYTHING
IS UNDER
CONTROL

=

A MEMOIR WITH RECIPES

PHYLLIS GRANT

FARRAR, STRAUS AND GIROUX

NEW YORK

Farrar, Straus and Giroux
120 Broadway, New York 10271

Library of Congress Cataloging-in-Publication Data
Names: Grant, Phyllis, author.
Title: Everything is under control : a memoir with recipes /
    Phyllis Grant.
Description: First edition. | New York : Farrar, Straus and
    Giroux, [2020]
Identifiers: LCCN 2019056121 | ISBN 9780374150143
    (hardcover)
Subjects: LCSH: Grant, Phyllis. | Women cooks—United
    States—Biography. | Cooks—United States—Biography. |
    Mothers and daughters—United States—Biography.
Classification: LCC TX910.5.G725 A3 2020 | DDC
    641.5092 [B]—dc23
LC record available at https://lccn.loc.gov/2019056121

Our books may be purchased in bulk for promotional, educational, or
business use. Please contact your local bookseller or the Macmillan
Corporate and Premium Sales Department at 1-800-221-7945, extension
5442, or by e-mail at MacmillanSpecialMarkets@macmillan.com.

www.fsgbooks.com
www.twitter.com/fsgbooks • www.facebook.com/fsgbooks

For Matthew

. . . the rhythm will keep me awake, changing.

—ROBERT HASS

EVERYTHING
IS UNDER
CONTROL

Here, there is no intense heat.

I whack the cold dough with my rolling pin.

There is no Chef.

I lean all my weight into the flattened disc.

No dupes.

Roll, spin, quick flip, flour, exhale.

There is no judgment. No sweat. No VIPs.

My heart starts to race.

There are only my children, perched on stools, trying to control their eager hands, excited to fill their hungry bellies.

=

When my great-grandfather, on my mother's side, dies of myasthenia gravis, his business partner takes everything and my great-grandmother falls into a year of anxiety and deep depression. She goes away to a sanatorium while her daughter, my grandmother Phyllis, lives with relatives.

My great-grandmother finally moves back home and takes two jobs in order to make ends meet. While she drives a school bus and works as an ophthalmologist's assistant, my grandmother Phyllis is in charge of meals. There is no Hamburger Helper. No takeout. No frozen pizza. So she learns to cook. She is ten.

=

Wait. Assembly line. Please cut all the apples in half before you start peeling them.

But why, Mom? My son wants to do it his way.

My daughter eye-rolls in his direction. She understands. She keeps her closet color-coordinated and her socks in a neat little row.

She smiles. I smile back. And then I cut myself.

As my daughter wraps my finger in a Band-Aid, I tell my kids about how I used to cut myself several times a week when I worked in restaurants. Sometimes a little nick, sometimes a gushing wound that three Band-Aids and a finger cot could not contain. How I would squat down behind the lockers, my hand wrapped in a bloody apron, begging my finger to stop bleeding so I could get back to my station before the Chef saw that I was gone.

My son speed-climbs up onto my hip, charmingly invading my personal space in the way only a five-year-old can.

But why were you embarrassed?

I place him a safe distance away on the counter and nestle the sliced apples down into the hot sugar and butter.

Because I knew nothing, my love.

I wrap the dough up on the rolling pin and unroll it out over the apples, quickly tucking the edges down with a butter knife. My chest tightens and starts to ache.

But now you know everything.

I don't correct him.

=

My grandmother Phyllis marries a painter who likes his gin, his Mozart, his cigarettes. And so does she. They settle in Berkeley, California, with their two kids, where she continues cooking the inexpensive comfort foods of her youth. Tough cuts of lamb become stew. Stale bread is for cheese toasts or croutons. Ham hock flavors a pot of split pea soup that lasts for days. Eggs are baked in ramekins or scrambled or turned into soufflés. There is no waste.

While there is a formality to things—napkin in your lap, no milk bottles on the table, don't eat over the sink—the table is also the easiest place to be. No rushing. No shortcuts. Every meal counts.

=

My daughter opens the oven door. I slide in the tarte tatin. She goes back to her homework world. My son and I sit on the dirty floor in front of the oven and wait.

Mom, there's a problem.

What?

Mom, I don't think I can look at you and say what I'm thinking.

I pull him into my lap and cradle his impossibly long body, carefully covering his eyes with my hands. I feel his heart racing in his eyelids.

Mom, I don't want to die.

Did you know that we all die?

No we don't. Not the Easter Bunny or Santa Claus.

But they're all crazy full of magic.

I just don't know how it will feel to die.

He nuzzles his face in the crook of my arm, smearing dirt, snot, tears on my sleeve. We hold hands and rock.

=

My grandmother Elizabeth, on my father's side, grows up in Minnesota with a mother who can create a meal out of a seemingly empty cupboard and a dairyman father who spends hours tending to his cheeses, coaxing and trimming with his special knife, storing them all in a dedicated refrigerator. Elizabeth's brother is eighteen years older, so she lives the life of an only child. She teaches herself to paint.

=

Mom, when is the tarte tatin done?

When the puff pastry is light brown and firm and the caramel is bubbling like crazy.

Mom, that sounds dangerous.

=

My grandparents meet in a senator's office in Washington, D.C. She is twenty-one. He is a thirty-year-old journalist from Dothan, Alabama, who chooses his words carefully, doesn't suffer fools, and is incredibly proper. They raise my dad and his two siblings in Bethesda, Maryland, where my grandmother Elizabeth moves like a hummingbird, keeping their world house-tour beautiful. She is a reluctant cook who would much rather be painting or gardening or designing intricate tablescapes with white birds. The house is filled with politicians and neighbors and highballs and cheeseballs and shrimp hanging off crystal bowls. Dinner, which waits in the oven for the lengthy cocktail hour to wind down, is often a variation on a dish they call Super Supper Slush: canned beans, corn, and tomatoes casseroled and then baked until bubbling.

=

Dude, do you want to watch me flip the tarte tatin?

His face lights up.

As I invert it onto a cake plate, I splash hot caramel all over my hands, the table, the floor, my son's shoes.

ShitcrapfuckIamsosorryareyouallrightIamsuchanidiotareyou allrightIcannotbelieveIdidthat.

Mom, I'm fine.

I jumped the gun.

You did what with a gun?

=

My parents meet in college. They share a love of music. They fight every day about the Vietnam War; my mom is full-bore against it. My father slowly comes around to her ways. They get married and move to the North Beach area of San Francisco, where my dad rides a motorcycle and my mom learns from the downstairs neighbors how to make whole-grain bread. Six flights up, they push my younger brother and me on a swing—through the fog, over a roof garden filled with herbs and citrus trees— precariously close to the edge.

My mom starts a catering company. My dad starts a management consulting company. Money is always tight. They buy a fixer-upper in Berkeley. On the weekend, my father is on his back fixing plumbing or hanging off the side of the house slowly shingling.

My mom goes back to school to study acting, so she teaches my dad the two things she thinks he needs to know to take over cooking dinner: the proportions for vinaigrette and how to roast chicken. Every night, while watching Walter Cronkite, he teaches himself to cook. He is thirty-five.

From then on, they cook together. Thanks to the Cuisinart, the bread maker, the pasta machine, Julia Child, and a garden of salad greens and parsley and lemons and avocados, there is a perpetual swirl of homemade fettuccini with butter and Parmesan, butter lettuce salads with shallot vinaigrette, glazed lemon cakes, and so much chicken.

=

When I am eleven years old, I lose fifteen pounds. Everyone looks for a reason. Blood tests, weekly weigh-ins, X-rays, intense parental discussions behind closed doors. It is 1981 and people aren't talking about appetite, hormones, and the teenage brain. They rule out the big stuff like anorexia and brain tumors. All I know is I keep looking and I just can't find any hunger in my body.

On weekend mornings, I bake. I bake to feed others. Danish ebelskiver, Belgian waffles, French toast, crêpes, chocolate chip cookies, bûches de Noël.

When I cook, I am calm. And confident. Baking works. You just follow the rules. There is comfort in the logic.

=

Often, in the middle of dinner, I slide down under the kitchen table and snuggle with the dog. As I listen to the muffled voices and clinking of glasses, my head gets all bubbly and blissful. I close my eyes and I am on a brightly lit stage pirouetting, suspending, leaping. I can't stop choreographing dances in my head.

After a year, I start eating again. I am twelve.

=

My best friend and I sit on the kitchen counter, eating toasted presliced Colombo San Francisco sourdough, discussing our intersecting dreams of bigger sticker collections, kissing Han Solo, getting an apartment together in New York City, world peace. Each slice of toast drips with butter and my mom's apricot jam. There is no such thing as being full.

=

Left leg up up up. Toes to the sky. I am fourteen, in my attic bedroom in front of the full-length mirror, surrounded by magazine cutouts of Rob Lowe, the Soloflex man, and all the actors from *Fame*. I slam down into a standing split. Over and over again.

I don't see myself. I see only the dancer I want to become.

=

My mom and I get out of the cab at Ninety-Third and Broadway, stand on the sidewalk, and look seven flights up to my new home: a residence hotel filled with Juilliard students.

She walks into the apartment ahead of me and takes it all in. Stained rug. Bedroom windows facing an air shaft. No kitchen.

We decide that the top of a left-behind yellow dresser will be my kitchen counter. My mom opens a drawer and finds used syringes. She throws them in the trash without comment and takes me shopping for my first winter in New York City.

I sit down on the floor of Bloomingdale's in an ocean of winter coats. They all look the same. It is 1988. There are lots of shoulder pads. I don't know how to choose.

My mom picks out a black wool coat, a floral scarf, a whisk, two wooden spoons, a plastic spatula, a cheese grater, a hot plate, and a microwave.

We eat all over the city. Cheesecake and French fries and mesclun salads with goat cheese. Chocolate sundaes. Tiramisu. Sun-dried tomatoes are everywhere. Nothing is seasonal, everything is overpriced and oversize and over-packaged and over the top. We eat so we don't have to acknowledge what's coming next. But every time I look up, she confirms—with a gaze, a smile, an arm squeeze—that I am just where I need to be. And then I need to look away.

She flies back to Berkeley, leaving me in my kitchen-less one-bedroom apartment with a membership to the Museum of Modern Art and a book of her handwritten recipes.

=

We are so hungry.

We dance all day long. In the studios. In the stairwells. On the sofas in the lounge. Down Broadway. It is my childhood dream come to life. The New York City package: 1988 style. Dance school. Depressing apartment. Leg warmers. Straw basket bag like Coco on *Fame*.

There are no dorms. We don't know how to cook. New York City is our cafeteria.

White onion, cheddar, and tomato omelets with French fries in fluorescent diners, all-you-can-eat barbecue ribs at Dallas BBQ, General Tso's chicken with free white wine, Ben & Jerry's New York Super Fudge Chunk ice cream, banana muffins with inch-thick streusel, airy blueberry scones, Häagen-Dazs bars, Doritos, and Peanut M&M's.

We don't care what we eat. We just want to be full so we can do it all again the next day.

=

My nightly soundtrack is made up of car alarms, a hissing radiator, and the frantic inhales and exhales of my assigned roommate trying to climb the walls. Several times a week, she puts in a James Taylor tape and run run run slams her naked body against the wall, her hands and feet clawing at the chipped paint, sobbing as her body slides to the ground.

I meet her older brother. He has scars over a quarter of his body. Something about a backyard barbecue and an exploding can of lighter fluid and the death of an older sister. He asks me to watch out for his baby sister.

She tiptoes down the street as if she is walking on air, smiling hard at everyone, engaging strangers in conversations about the beautiful day, her light blue eyes brimming with tears, her ecstatic bliss changing midsentence to deep gloom.

She buys a folding shopping cart at Bed Bath & Beyond that she pushes up and down Broadway. She bursts through the door with a new collection of gathered items: a broken lamp, three packages of stale Mint Milanos for the price of one, a man she met at Tasti D-Lite frozen yogurt shop.

I shake her awake every day. I feed her granola. I tuck the hair behind her ears.

=

My ballet teacher squeezes my waist. He trained with Rudolf Nureyev and wears a cape that he flips back when he's angry. He smacks my ass with a stick.

Stop eating so many croissants, Phyllis.

He says I have an attitude problem. He would like me to disappear.

We share a bathroom with the School of American Ballet, I listen to the heaving in the stalls. I watch girls erase their femininity, their fertility.

I learn the tricks.

A stick of Juicy Fruit gum is ten calories and if you chew it for over an hour, you will burn eleven calories.

Bulimia is much harder to cover up. It's loud and messy. But you get to eat more. Anorexia is clean and requires control.

I choose anorexia.

Breakfast is coffee and a cigarette. Lunch is a cigarette. Dinner is broth.

I think I'm in control. I hear the words I want to hear: *You look great, Phyllis. Look at the line in your penché. You finally have a waist.*

I audition for the big performance at the Juilliard Theater. I don't even get cast as an understudy. I almost get cut in my first evaluation. So I ask why.

We saw a lot of potential in you but you haven't lived up to it. Your technique is very weak and we're not sure you're going to make it here at Juilliard.

I go to the Juilliard Halloween party. Alcohol hits my empty stomach. I don't remember getting carried out of the school and ten blocks up Broadway to my apartment. I don't remember how I get out of the tight green dress. I do remember waking up as my head slams the side of the bathtub, my body slumping to the tile floor.

=

Head down, purse pulled into body, face emotionally sealed, I move with the anonymous throngs up and down Broadway. I find a speed I never knew I had. I walk for distraction. I walk to try to understand what to do. I walk to try to figure out who I am. I am eighteen.

I visit every church, temple, mosque on the Upper West Side that will let me in. I breathe in the religious air. It feels thick, cool, supportive. It smells musty but sweet like my grandmother Elizabeth's garage. I pretend to believe in God by listening to the music, planting my feet on the cement floor, holding a Bible to my chest.

I peer into brownstones. I want to sit at those kitchen tables. I want to be fed. I buy a box of cake mix and make it in my microwave. To watch it rise. For the smell. To feel the warmth of just-baked anything in my hands.

=

Why don't you take your clothes off, Phyllis. Yes. Like that. Nice. And now do the splits. Beautiful. Let me photograph you from the other side. Hold on. Wow. I am so grateful to you. These photos will be so helpful. Now cup your breasts. Yes. That's it. Yes.

I am not the only Juilliard dancer who goes downtown to the Puck Building to have her picture taken in the anatomy teacher's special studio for his extracurricular project. None of us tell. We don't want to ruin his life.

=

My mother sends me newspaper clippings. Where to get the best tea. Lists of the best New York City restaurants. Farmers' market locations. Thanksgiving hotline numbers. Turkey cooking tips are highlighted: *You need half a cup of stuffing for each pound of bird*. Safety tips are circled: *Thyme has been shown to be active against salmonella*. How I need to check my turkey after two and a quarter hours. How much she will miss me at Thanksgiving this year. How my brother is growing an inch a week. How much she loves me.

But my first Thanksgiving away from home isn't in a home kitchen. It is a prix fixe dinner at Windows on the World at the top of One World Trade Center. Three young women. Three bottles of wine. Three courses consisting of gelatinous corn chowder, dry turkey with mucousy gravy, leaden apple pie. Two out of the three of us throw it all up in the fancy bathroom. Before we leave, I stand at the floor-to-ceiling windows, tracing the avenue lights straight back uptown to my new home. Here, 100 blocks south and 107 floors up, I am relieved to be so far away from it all.

=

I'm fine, Daddy. Everything is fine. I love you too.

I hang up the pay phone outside my apartment building, step over a homeless man, walk past the bullet hole in the lobby door, and take the stairs. A few flights up, I sit down. The stairwell stinks of piss and misery. The building around me vibrates with Bach, Madonna, and laughter.

I don't want what I thought I wanted. I don't want to decide what to eat. I don't want to be set free.

I light a cigarette and inhale menthol smoke as often and as deeply as one cigarette will allow, all for that two-second dopamine buzz that makes space in my brain for the belief that life won't always feel like this.

I am a very good dancer. But I will never be a great one.

All I want is to go home and eat my mom's roast chicken.

=

It's small. It's filled with roaches. It's coated with the stink and stickiness of the previous ten tenants. But it's mine. My first kitchen. With a gas stovetop and an oven with a broiler drawer. The freezer has a two-inch border of ice but it's big enough for two pints of ice cream for my new roommate and me. I have a place to collect condiments. I buy a dish towel and an apron. I open my mom's recipe book and follow her cursive through the chopping of the onion, the toasting of the rice, the never ever lifting of the lid until the timer goes off. I end up with a pot of brown rice. Her words work.

=

An actor or a stockbroker or a film director sits across from me at a diner or a bar or on a park bench reciting his overused script of *it's so nice to be out with a beautiful girl, you are so different, so special, so cultured.* And off we go to watch a foreign film or see an art exhibit at the Whitney or visit his favorite drama bookstore. We end up back at his teeny tiny apartment or black marble penthouse or West Side brownstone where we roll around and talk and roll around and talk, pressing body parts to body parts because sometimes that's enough. And then he reminds me of who is hanging over us: the beautiful homecoming queen or aspiring model who never ventures uptown or fiancée back in Charlotte. He says *I can't, I can't, I can't, I really shouldn't* until bam he lets go and says *she would probably be fine with us having sex because she is a very open girl* and in that moment I get mature and moral beyond my eighteen years and say *this is not right, let's just fall asleep and see how we feel in the morning.* I leave before he wakes up and do the walk of shame through Lincoln Center with my smeared mascara and the previous night's carefully chosen dress, feeling like the best person in the world because I've saved his relationship. I power through the forty blocks home with my light coffee and a slow-building regret: *why didn't I just sleep with him because at least I'd have that.*

=

For my second Thanksgiving away from home, I take the train to Pittsburgh to visit friends at Carnegie Mellon.

The air is bitingly cold. The landscape is bleak. The East Coast just feels fucked up.

But there is a comforting sameness to our failed romantic entanglements, our lack of focus, our existential angst. We have taken a few too many steps outside our comfortable worlds and we're all ready to run back home to California.

Their apartment is huge, two floors perched above a pizza parlor. The kitchen is large enough to comfortably accommodate our dysfunctional group. We fumble our way through planning our first Thanksgiving dinner. Even though I have never done this before, I find myself in charge.

Before bed, I tear up the challah so that it gets stale for the next day's stuffing. I study the map of recipes written by my mom. My entire childhood Thanksgiving experience is on paper. Mashed potatoes. Mincemeat pie. Creamed onions.

I can't sleep. I am scared to begin.

I get up early to take the turkey out of the fridge and bring it to room temperature. I dice onions and sauté them with a stick of butter. I add celery and seasonings, the stale bread, and chicken stock. I can hear my parents' and my grandparents' voices. *More salt. Taste. More liquid. Taste. More poultry seasoning. That's it. Now stop. The bread will soften. The turkey juices will flavor the stuffing. Don't overdo it.*

I carefully separate the turkey skin from the flesh, making room for slices of cold butter. I press the stuffing in both ends of the bird, sew it all up with large scrappy stitches, and wrap the string a few extra times around the ends of the drumsticks. Just in case. I don't want a blow-out. And then I tie a knot and hope for the best. It all feels very fragile, intimate.

But I don't know when it's done. How long it should rest. How to carve it. What's safe. What's dangerous. All the things that aren't written down on the recipe pages. I call my parents with questions every hour until the turkey is on the kitchen table.

=

He buzzes me in.

I walk up the lopsided stairs, hearing the clanking of dishes from each apartment, smelling three floors of family dinners.

He doesn't know that I have been crushing on him for weeks, following him around school, getting as close as I can on the stairs, trying to hear what he is listening to on his Walkman, once almost reaching out and touching his shirt.

He is waiting in the open door. I slip past him. I already love his faded Levi's, his white T-shirt, his smell.

There is no table, no bed. There are no chairs. Just French movie posters on the walls, a futon, a jar of tomato sauce in the kitchenette, a pile of Doc Martens in the corner, a stack of *The New York Times* that comes up to my knees.

I feel unsteady from the steaming furnace, the tilting floorboards, my racing heart.

We get stoned and watch *The Big Blue*, a movie with dolphins and deep-sea diving and Rosanna Arquette. Halfway through, he pauses the VCR.

Are you hungry, Phyllis?

I sit on the floor and watch him melt fourteen cloves of finely chopped garlic into olive oil. As he pours the jar of tomato sauce into the hot oil, it splatters up the white high-gloss kitchenette wall. He sets the floor with black plastic place mats and carefully folded cloth napkins.

The snow blows sideways past the windows. We fall asleep back to back, hands to ourselves.

=

Six weeks in and he is shaking.

Phyllis?

I am one large heart.

Matthew?

I get up early before dance class just to experience the in-love version of my morning routine. The sky is bluer. Cheese Danishes taste better. My grands jetés are higher.

＝

When we're not kissing, M and I talk about food.

We walk around the West Village and peek into the French bistros we can't afford.

We wait in line on the Upper West Side for over an hour to eat apple pancakes, buttermilk waffles with bacon, paprika home fries, and cream biscuits with strawberry butter.

We spend a week's worth of food money on a dozen ravioli filled with butternut squash and sage. We carefully boil the precious pillows and then drown them in garlicky tomato sauce.

=

I can't get through the Juilliard lobby fast enough. I wait for the elevator with musicians, their instruments glued to their bodies.

I throw *The New York Times* and a pack of Marlboro Lights down on my favorite corner table in the cafeteria and pull out the crisp food section. I don't want to read it yet because then it will be gone and I'll have to wait for another week.

I eat the streusel top off my enormous blueberry muffin and sip my light coffee. I look out at the yellow-cab blur at the intersection of Sixty-Sixth and Broadway. The morning light makes me hopeful. I finally let myself open the food section and flip through until I find the latest restaurant review. I read it over and over again.

I head one flight up to the dance studio and start my warm-up. As I demi-plié, demi-plié, grand plié, I am thinking only about grilled monkfish and chocolate soufflés with molten centers.

=

I walk through Manhattan with a warm six-month-old baby strapped to my chest. I walk to stay awake. I walk because that's what nannies do. Playing mom comes naturally to me, but parenting someone else's child is the loneliest of boredoms. I am twenty-two.

I tell the baby my thoughts on everything. The never-ending winter. How much I love the sticky buns at the bakery on Chambers Street. How bored I am with my café job selling hazelnut coffee and oat bran muffins. How frustrated I am by the previous day's audition.

I failed before I even walked into the room.

The tenth one I've been to since I graduated from Juilliard. How they pin a piece of paper to my chest. How one small group at a time, we walk out into the middle of the room. How the producers have us turn to face the back of the room so they can see the shapes of our asses.

So humiliating, little one.

Pirouettes on the right. And the left. And then they teach us the audition sequence. How I step out into the middle of the room. How my mind goes blank.

I panicked. I ran up Broadway. All the way home.

I stop under a passenger bridge that straddles two buildings and stare up at an airy loft filled with a life that I think I want.

Someday, I will have morning glories weaving up my very own fire escape.

My rocking and yammering have put the baby to sleep. I turn the corner and see models and lawyers and Wall Streeters slipping out of limos and into a restaurant. I sneak in the front door. The air smells fancy, fermented.

I leave before anyone sees me and go around to the back. Cooks slip out to lean against the brick wall, to take quick drags of cigarettes. They all seem rushed and guilty. Each opening of the kitchen door lets me sneak a peek into their bright world.

I watch an army of cooks in crisp white shirts and aprons, red-faced, sweating, barking out orders, heads down, arms reaching and stirring, plucking herbs and flipping fish and testing sauces with tasting spoons.

The industrial kitchen fan pumps a mash-up of lunch fumes out into the alley.

I want my hair to smell like chocolate and garlic and fish.

I want to lean in and carefully place the roasted beets next to the potato purée.

I want a purpose.

I rock the baby, hugging him tight, his back to my belly. All I want is to unstrap him, hand him to the next person walking by, enter the kitchen, and never look back.

=

M and I have been together for three years. For my twenty-third birthday, we indulge in a four-hour restaurant marathon of Belon oysters, rabbit, pigeon and foie gras wrapped in Savoy cabbage, quince purée, eggplant and goat cheese terrine, wild striped bass, monkfish, lobster with vanilla bean, sweetbreads, snippy discussions about the actress who keeps leaving M poems on the drama board, venison, potato purée, crème fraîche, balsamic reduction, quark and chocolate and passion fruit soufflés, a solo walk around the block, crème brûlée, angry tears, pine nut tarts, Concord grape and chocolate sorbets, hand-holding, prune Armagnac and vanilla bean ice creams, the tracing of M's life lines on his palm, three tiers of petit fours, homemade chocolates, more tears, Sauternes, a staggering bill.

We cab home. I try to kiss M. He says he might throw up on me. He is so full. I am so altered.

M guides my body down until the back of my head rests in his lap. I bend my knees and tuck my feet under me. Midtown flashes by. He gently drags his fingers through my hair. I tell him I want to be a chef.

＝

When my grandmother Phyllis is working full-time toward her Ph.D. in psychology, my mom does much of the cooking. She is seventeen.

She and my grandmother mutually mark up the margins of *Joy of Cooking*, *Mastering the Art of French Cooking*, and *The Fannie Farmer Cookbook*. TOO RICH. ADD EXTRA VANILLA. LESS SUGAR. MORE SALT. DON'T OVERMIX. GREAT RECIPE! GOOD FOR A LARGE GROUP. BLAND.

=

Every day, after work at the café, I continue cooking my way through Lindsey Shere's *Chez Panisse Desserts*, Julia Child's *The Way to Cook*, *The Culinary Institute of America Cookbook*, and Rose Levy Beranbaum's *The Cake Bible*.

On the weekends, I volunteer at a French bakery, writing down everything I see and hear.

Wait for the flourless chocolate cakes to rise, drop, and then crack.

Warm the egg whites before beating for greater volume.

Wait for the sponge cake to pull away from the sides of the sheet pan.

The lemon cake is done if it springs back when you press it with your finger.

Knock on the bread to see if it sounds hollow.

I think I am ready for a restaurant kitchen.

=

I am in the way.

Hot behind you.

Everyone is yelling.

Coming through. On your left.

It's my first day as a pastry assistant at a large restaurant that has one of the busiest lunch services in Midtown. Lawyers and agents fill the tables. Arugula salads and chicken breasts stuffed with goat cheese fill their plates.

Pick. Up. Pick up now. And eighty-six the foie.

While plating desserts, the Pastry Chef tells me what to do.

When you're done with lunch service, please bake off the chocolate chip cookies. You will need to peel and core a minimum of twenty apples a day. I'll talk you through the tarte tatin when we have a little more time. For the ice cream custard, you'll find the chinois and the bain-marie downstairs by the walk-in. Oh, and the 10x is in the pantry next to the linens. Oui, Chef! VIP desserts coming up. Pick up table ten!!!! Fuck. I need some runners. Would you bring me a few hotel pans? Someone keeps taking my stash.

I don't understand.

Read off the dupes for me, will you? I want to make sure we have enough cheesecake to get through service. How many all day?

I am panicking.

How. Many. Cheesecakes.

She points to the tickets that are lined up above the pastry station.

I try to decipher the scribbles. *Five cheesecakes?*

She double-checks the orders.

Five. Yes. All day. That's right. You should put your hair back or Chef will say something inappropriate. Buy some boots or clogs. Something with a hard toe. Knives fall.

She yells to the dishwasher: *Por favor. Can you wash tres sheet pans? For the new girl. She has a thousand cookies to make. Gracias. Oh, and Phyllis, please chop these pecans while I get some family meal. You want some? Looks pretty decent today.*

I ask where I can find the knives to chop the nuts.

You don't have your own knives?

I stop asking questions.

=

Six months in and I have experienced the obscenely long hours and witnessed the fire hazards, rampant drug use, and misogynistic everything. I have also learned that I am allergic to flour when it's in the air, which is constant in the pastry room. I sneeze a lot.

I still want this more than ever.

On my day off, I go back to the restaurant where M and I had the marathon meal. I eat lunch and drink enough wine to work up the courage to meet the Pastry Chef. He invites me into the kitchen and shows me around. I ask him if he is hiring. He tells me to call the following week. I do. Nothing. I call the next week. Nothing. I call every Friday for three months. And then:

Phyllis. Thanks for calling. Someone just quit. Can you start Monday?

=

I float up on my tippy-toes, lengthen my arms as far as they will go, and reach up to the highest rack of the pastry oven to check on the mini tart shells. My jaw is tight. My stomach is a circle of knots. It is my third day working in pastry. The fish line watches me.

I hear she's a ballet dancer.

The shells are held in place with small weights to keep them from puffing up into balloons. I tip the sheet pan toward my face. I can almost see. Just one more inch, just a bit more, I almost have it.

The heavy sheet pan is more than I can support. A hot mess of dough and metal slides down my body—the tumbling avalanche so loud the entire kitchen stops and stares. I drop down to the ground to clean up, burning my fingertips over and over again as I pick up the weights.

=

I hike my pink bike up on my shoulder and walk down the stairs to the basement.

I pass a line cook and ask him what kind of fish he is carrying. *Can't talk, can't talk, can't talk, Chef needs this now, Felicia. Sorry.*

A prep guy squeezes past me, hugging a large bag of mesclun to his body.

The dishwasher—covered in sweat and grease and a mist of dirty water—leaps up the stairs two at a time with a stack of sheet pans.

Someone is always running.

A dozen voices welcome me: *Felicia!* They are The Family. They wash every vegetable that hits every plate. They scrub the floors. They lift the heaviest pots. They clean up the vomit in the bathrooms, in the hall, on the sidewalk. They fix the mistakes.

There is always too much to do.

I shove my bike in the storage room behind flats of eggplants and tomatoes and raspberries that need to be inventoried. The chef shirts have fallen down into a puddle of dirty water. There is a large clean one on top. I remove my sweatshirt and quickly button the scratchy starchy white shirt up over my white tank top and sports bra. I pull down the remaining chef pants from the top shelf. All extra-smalls.

Fuck. Fuck. Fuck.

I dig through my locker and find a large pair of chef pants tucked behind my work boots. I tear off a three-foot piece of plastic wrap, swing it behind me like a jump rope, pull it into my lower back, and yank the two ends out in front of me until they won't stretch anymore. I thread it through the belt loops and tie the ends into a plastic bow. My body is hidden. I can work.

=

I listen.

Chef lives at the flat top next to the pass. He barely lifts his head. He moves his arms over pots and plates, glancing up to motion to a cook to bring the sauce, or flashing two fingers in response to *How long on the bass?*

I live twenty feet away in pastry.

Chef speaks softly but his voice travels across the fish line, down the pastry line, over the roar of the convection oven, straight into my ear.

Felicia, what did you do last night?

I can't even remember what day it is. I yank the sleeves of

my chef shirt down to hide dozens of red, blistery burns that line my inner arms.

Felicia, I'm going to need passion fruit for the VIP fish dish.

Oui, Chef.

Full-tilt run downstairs to the walk-in refrigerator. I close the heavy metal door and sit down on an overturned plastic bucket. The piercingly cold air slips through my nostrils and down into my lungs, making me cough. I eat a handful of raspberries from Chile.

For the hundredth time that day, I tell myself that I am not cut out for this, that I am not strong enough, that I shouldn't be here. I plan my escape: I will take a right at the top of the stairs instead of a left. I will head north up the alley, underneath the passenger bridge, and walk all the way home. No one will notice.

I hear someone opening the door and I remember why I am here. I lift up the bottom corners of my apron, fill the cloth with a dozen passion fruit, fly out of the walk-in, up the stairs, and make a left back into the kitchen.

＝

Chef watches almost every single dish go out at the pass. And then he wants to see the plates as they come back. If a customer leaves behind more than a few bites of her dish, the server will get questioned. *Is she just full? Did you ask her if she liked it? Please go find out.*

We are all caught up in Chef's meticulousness. The pressure to deliver the perfect pine nut tart, the freshest ice cream, the loveliest berries, an impeccable tower of petit fours. That service, that hour, that minute, that dupe; it all matters more than anything in the world.

=

Out of the blue one night, after three months of working in pastry, Chef puts me on the fish line. I don't talk, I just follow the hands of the cook on my left, using my fingers to press the pink skin of the rainbow trout down into the searing hot oil in the pan. Just as the flesh turns opaque at the edges, a quick flip and it's done. Right onto the plate with toasted pine nuts, mesclun, and sweet balsamic dressing. And then twenty more. And then they need me back in pastry.

I feel like I'm on the wrong side. I want the heat. I want to touch the food more.

Three months later, I ask Chef if he would consider moving me out of pastry and over to garde-manger.

=

We line up shoulder to shoulder with our plastic cutting boards secured on moist kitchen towels, our faces locked and focused, our knives a frenzied militaristic blur, chopping the vegetables that The Family has just cleaned.

The basement radio is cranked so high that we can't hear our own breath. We just feel the music vibrating in our bones, the Spanish lyrics so loud and familiar and thought-obliterating that we all fall into line and get shit done.

Chef hovers, watching our technique, so close I can smell his aftershave, so close I can feel his breath on my neck. Goose bumps travel down my triceps.

Felicia, you are a mess.

I retie my plastic-wrap belt, smooth out my apron, and wipe down my cutting board. As I chop my way down a bunch of chives with my left hand, I copy my neighbor's technique: blade at a slant, fingers tucked under. My thumb cramps.

You are bruising the chives.

Oui, Chef.

And you look really tired.

A server taps me on the shoulder. *Felicia, first order is in.*

I pack up my knife bag, stack the quart containers of prep on a sheet pan, and bound up the stairs to my garde-manger station.

=

The morning prep guy is making the salad dressing in my station. His alcohol stench is more powerful than usual and makes me gag. As I unroll my knife bag, he reaches around me for the olive oil, his firm crotch pressing up to my ass, his breath exhaling into my ear. I push him off. As he squats down to place the salad dressing in the open low-boy refrigerator, his fingers trail down along my hamstring, knee, calf, his strong hand landing firmly around my ankle.

I look down and ask him about his wife and kids. He snaps at me: *Hurry up, Felicia, you are always late.*

On this, he is right. I am always late. I didn't used to be. I have been working in garde-manger for what feels like years. But when I count the days, it's fewer than thirty.

I miss the Pastry Chef. I miss the chocolate soufflés. I miss scooping quenelles of ice cream. I miss the relative calm. I want to step it back. I don't want this version.

=

I bang out the remaining prep: chopped chives, parsley, and shallots. Once the dupes roll in, I can do nothing but plate.

I lug buckets of oysters up from the basement and stack enough plates for the first twenty orders. I plug in my mini burner, retie my plastic-wrap belt, and ignore the electric ache that has been flashing in my heart every day this week before service.

Without hesitation or self-doubt, the extern next to me brunoises the carrots for the soup and then juliennes the fennel for my salad. He's only here for a few months. So helpful. So careful. So skilled. So ready to fly out the door the moment he can. He freaks when I borrow his knife. *Careful. Phyllis. Wait. You never slide the knife edge across the cutting board. It will fuck up the edge.* He lends me a copy of Marco Pierre White's *White Heat*. He wants to be a rock-and-roll chef. I just want to make it through the next dinner service.

=

Chef sneaks up behind me and tickles my lower back. He gently pulls my ponytail.

You look like a cheerleader today, Felicia.

He pulls yellowtail out of my low-boy refrigerator and asks me to smell it.

No smell, Chef.

He picks up one of my knives and slices off a piece of the fish to prepare a dish for a VIP. Without looking up, he says, *Felicia, your knives are never sharp enough.*

Oui, Chef.

He shifts his weight from side to side, mumbling to himself, furrowing his brow, components moving together as if he's gathering ideas from the air. He does this every service. I only know how to follow a recipe. But he is making shit up as he goes along. And I love watching.

He whisks together crème fraîche, fromage blanc, sherry wine vinegar, chopped chives, almond oil, salt, pepper. *Never stop tasting, Felicia.*

He scoops some up with his finger to taste. I do the same. And then I wait for the next step. Sweat drips down the backs of my legs and into my boots.

Do you have some blanched beans?

Oui, Chef. Fava, lima, Romano, yellow wax, haricots verts.

All of them, please.

I follow his every move so that I can repeat the dish over and over again throughout the evening. The way he examines the beans, gently cradling them in his fingers before dropping each one down into the bowl. How he coats everything with the creamy, nutty mixture by quickly shifting the bowl away from his body and yanking back, away and back, away and back, as if he's flipping a crêpe. I watch his hands. The path of his eyes. Tossing, tasting, adjusting. This is when I breathe. This is when I learn.

The first order comes in. My chest gets all warm and prickly. Sweat pools in my bra. I yank my ponytail up into a tight bun and fall off a cliff for seven hours.

=

*F*elicia?

I feel Chef's voice in my hands.

No, no, no, no, please, not now, I mumble to myself.

I run over to the pass. It is 6:00 p.m. and the expeditor is already drenched in sweat.

Servers in starched shirts and bow ties line the mirrored wall. The first rush hasn't hit. They look around for something to talk about.

Chef steps away from the pass, turning his back on the yelling expeditor.

Chef, we're waiting on the cod. Come on!

Chef places food in front of my face, expecting my lips to part.

Merde, someone bring me a cod!

Chef's warm fingers slide into my mouth. I close my eyes so I don't have to watch everyone watching me.

Everything is up! Wipe the plates!

I yank my head away, giving Chef's salty fingertips only a quick swipe from the inside of my upper lip, promising myself this is all he'll ever get.

The servers pick opal basil and lemon thyme from dozens of potted herbs that line the mirrored wall opposite the pass.

Let's go.

Garnish on. Plates up.

Table ten.

They move toward the dining room.

Rattlesnake coats my tongue.

=

Felicia, finito la musica?

Sí.

The dishwashers scrub the floor around me as I put lids on all the quart containers, wrap up the yellowtail, check that there is enough salad dressing for the next day's lunch. It's 1:00 a.m. Service is over. I take advantage of the empty fish flat tops and start cooking slices of eggplant for the vegetable terrine in a dozen sauté pans.

I wander into the empty dining room holding a gold-rimmed china plate filled with found scraps: sliced venison, cold potato purée, overcooked chocolate soufflé.

I return to the kitchen, add a little more oil to the pans, flip the eggplant, and head back out to a padded Baroque chair. I pour myself wine from a deserted bottle. I wonder what it would be like to have enough money to just leave your wine behind.

I flip the eggplant again.

I pick up my wine and walk into the clean air-conditioned customer bathroom. I look in the mirror—at the bags under my eyes, the zits on my chin, the sallowness of my skin—and quickly turn away.

I head back to the kitchen for another hour. Creamy, sweet eggplant only comes with time.

=

I crouch down, lift up the back of my chef shirt, and cool my lower back on a stainless steel low-boy. I smile up at my friend on the meat line.

Do you have any lamb popsicles available?

Oui, Felicia. For you, anything.

Will you sharpen my knives?

Nope.

You suck.

Will you bike to Brooklyn with me this weekend, Felicia?

Oui.

I watch him open his oven and poke all the different cuts of meat.

How do you know when that one is done?

The pigeon? When it's firm like an excited woman's breast.

I need to quit.

He nods.

=

I run into Chef on the stairs.

Chef, can we talk?

I want to tell him that I wake up crying.

Felicia, taste this wine.

I want to tell him that I fall asleep crying.

Chef, I've been thinking really hard about something.

I want to tell him that I am mortified when he sends a fancy glass of wine over to me and only me in front of the whole kitchen.

He wraps my hand around a glass of wine. *Do you like this wine?*

I want to tell him that he shouldn't have moved me to garde-manger. That I wasn't ready. That I can't handle the six-day workweeks, the fifteen-hour days on my feet. That I may never be able to handle it.

I hand back the glass of wine. *Chef, I have to leave. I am giving you my two-week notice.*

Please leave my kitchen tonight.

He walks down the stairs. I walk up.

I throw my cooking boots into the dumpster and bike home. Feeling light. Feeling lost.

I take a shower, scrubbing my body until it burns, trying to remove the restaurant from my hair, my skin, under my nails.

I wrap my naked body around a sleeping M.

=

I get a job working lunch service at a Japanese restaurant. Most days, I bust out hundreds of desserts in under three hours. While the rushes are huge, the pressure is low. The VIPs haven't come for my desserts; they want the sashimi salad and the gold-flecked kampachi and the miso-marinated black cod. I am happily tucked away in my pastry station piping cursive bittersweet chocolate *Happy Birthday*s and carving kiwis into flowers and scooping yuzu sorbet. It's just a job. It pays well. I sleep well. I don't take any of it home. I have stopped crying. I have time to think about the rest of my life.

=

M and I separate the Tone Loc from the Madonna. The George Michael from the Mozart. The Cure from the Kate Bush.

After seven years, I want to know who I am without a partner.

We separate the KitchenAid from the amplifier. The Shakespeare from the David Foster Wallace.

I want to kiss other people.

We separate the *Diet for a Small Planet* from the *Desserts for Dummies*. The Luc Besson from the John Hughes. The bong from the tea strainer.

I live alone for the first time in my life. My West Village apartment. My dirty toilet. My *New York Times*. My neighbor who beats on the ceiling when he's drunk and irritated by my 3:00 a.m. vacuuming. My nasturtiums on the fire escape. My Con Ed bill. My Advil. My bed. My loneliness.

=

I turn away from the flat top to grab a sheet pan filled with ramekins. The tip of the sushi chef's blade slides through my pants, right above my left knee, in and out of my leg quickly, smoothly, cleanly.

At first, I feel nothing.

I'm so sorry, Sakura.

Blood starts trickling down my calf and into my boot.

No problem. I am fine.

Then comes the pain.

Just twenty minutes before, I spied on him while he

sharpened this knife. I wanted a lesson. But I was too shy to ask.

I turn the flame off from underneath the ginger crème brûlée custard and run into the customer bathroom. I tear my chef pants off above the knee. The restaurant manager hands me cash and puts me in a cab. I enter the emergency room and hear screams. I step over streaks of blood. There's a group of cops who just watched a man get thrown through a glass table and they're all hanging around to see if he survives. Four hours later, a doctor checks me out. *No stitches necessary,* he says as he tapes me up with crosshatched Band-Aids, *just watch out for those chefs.*

=

Round one. A chef. He sticks his tongue down my throat while pressing my bare back up against the metal grating of a closed bodega. He has a girlfriend. He promises to call me the next day. I listen to "Lightning Crashes" by Live for forty-eight hours straight. He never calls. Round one, over.

A date. A drink. A walk. He's gay and he doesn't know it. No more round two.

He is my writing teacher. He takes me out to dinner after class. He feeds me pasta and red wine. He touches my inner knee, he twirls my hair, he holds my cheeks. He tells me stories about hanging out with Allen Ginsberg and Jack Kerouac. He has done this too many times.

He's a comedian. He invites me to meet his friends, go skiing, move in. All on the first date. Round four. Over.

He wants to start a writing group. He is getting divorced. I can feel his loneliness through the phone. I don't call him back. No more round five.

He tells me he loves how I look reading Philip Roth on the reclining bicycle at the gym. That he is attracted to my long neck, to my serious face, to the fact that I wouldn't give him my phone number the first time we met. I can't believe how much he likes to talk about food. How much he likes to drink gin. How pillowy his lips feel. I decide to cook risotto for him. For a little while, there is no round seven.

=

I am twenty-six years old, at Columbia University, sitting next to very confident eighteen-year-olds.

I don't know how to e-mail or take notes or write a paper. I only know how to do triple pirouettes and press dough into a tart shell. But I have decided to get another undergraduate degree.

I read the dictionary before going to sleep, hoping the new words will stick in my brain. Paucity, pith, hegemony, trope, atavism, hyperbole, dogma, trifecta. I try out the words. In papers about James Joyce. In bad poetry about regret and lost love and femininity. In handwritten letters to M that I never send.

=

I run into M outside the Christopher Street subway station. He is so excited because he is going to Los Angeles for a month to star in a sitcom pilot.

As I watch his lips move, all I can think is how I miss waiting for the subway with my head on his shoulder. I miss the way he tucks his fists under his chin while he sleeps. I miss walking into a party with him.

He asks about my world. My freelance cookbook editing. My writing.

I miss his Kate Bush CD. I miss watching *Thirtysomething* reruns. I miss his hand on top of my head when I can't sleep. I miss kissing his cheekbones. I miss how hard he makes me laugh.

I tell him I want to be a yoga teacher. He looks confused. We are used to making these big career decisions together, not playing rapid-fire catch-up on a street corner.

I miss making him dinner.

We hug goodbye and then we kiss and we kiss and we kiss. It feels sneaky and new. And then he walks east and I walk west.

=

M comes home from Los Angeles and invites me over for dinner. I walk into his East Village ground-floor apartment and smile. His world minus my world looks like Greece. Everything is white: the curtains, the floors, the sheets, the plates, the towels.

His upstairs neighbor starts to sob uncontrollably. He tells me she does this every evening. He starts spending one night a week at my place. And then several nights a week. And then it's as if we never lived apart.

=

My grandmother Elizabeth proposes to my grandfather two weeks after they meet. He is too polite to say no.

=

Will you go on a honeymoon with me to Elba?

M puts down his silverware and stares at me.

Are you asking me to marry you?

I look down at the food on my plate. I can't eat. I have made our favorite dinner: lamb popsicles, crunchy hearts of romaine, avocado bowls. I have spent more money on the wine than we can afford and drunk most of the bottle on my own. He takes another bite, as if the meditative chewing allows him to sift this idea through his body.

He stops eating and moves over to the sofa. I rest my forehead on the table and wonder what I have done. He has always said there is no reason to get married. That he loves me. That I love him. That living together again is enough. I lift my head.

We can have a big dinner party. With all our friends and family.

He is so still. He is so stunned. He goes to bed.

He thinks about it for a few days.

=

I now pronounce you wife and husband. Phyllis, you may kiss the groom.

I rise up onto my barefoot tippy-toes and kiss him hard. With tongue.

And then we eat twelve cakes.

=

We spend the morning looking downtown. There are no cars. They come later: driving too fast, speeding uptown, filled with people in suits covered in ash.

First there are the mysterious flames.

Must have been a small plane.

We zoom in on the falling debris with binoculars and video cameras.

Must be papers. Can't be bodies.

A second explosion.

Our eyes move from one flaming building to the other.

The South Tower starts to fall from the sky—a silent, slow-motion top-to-bottom erasure, claps of dust billowing in all directions—until all that's left is a swath of blue September sky.

Some scream. Some point in disbelief. Some spin in circles. Some drop to the ground.

I take off running. Away from what I'm seeing. M chases me down, catching me from behind, pinning my arms in toward my center as you would a tantrumy child. He guides me back to the crowd. We try to hold the North Tower up in the sky with our eyes. And then it falls. This time M lets me run.

We huddle in our apartments, windows closed against the 24/7 sirens and acrid smoke. Our throats burn, our eyes sting, helicopters pulse in our eardrums all night long. We pick up the paper every morning and read the names. We all know someone.

I braise meat, assemble pesto lasagnas, bake chocolate chip cookies. All I can do is feed people.

Three weeks later, we tape an American flag to the side of our car and drive out of New York City.

We barrel all the way to California, moving fast toward something new.

=

*G*et the chef knife.

It is under our bed. We are lying in the dark in our funky Venice Beach rental bungalow, listening to the creaks, counting all the points of entry, imagining our imminent deaths. We are used to New York City with the triple-locked front doors and windows with security bars. In Los Angeles, we feel exposed and vulnerable.

Then the sun comes up and we do what we came to Los Angeles to do. M auditions for acting jobs. I teach yoga in strip malls. We pretend New York City isn't our everything.

At the farmers' market, we buy bags of arugula and kale. We sit on the curb, with iced coffees and five-grain scones, and watch the people walk by. For lunch, we toss the greens with pesto vinaigrette, top them with avocado and salmon, and eat out on our front stoop in the quiet, in the dry heat.

We haven't maxed out our credit cards yet. We don't see the traffic and the smog. We are oblivious to the mold that is climbing up the walls behind our sofa, creeping down the arms of my winter coats in the back of the closet, lining the kitchen cupboards, making our noses itch.

It's seventy degrees. In January. After twelve years in New York City, we just turn our faces up to the sun.

=

I can't stop eating quesadillas filled with Monterey Jack, topped with avocado, sour cream, jalapeño pickles.

My skin has never been so clear, my eyes have never been so bright.

Dutch babies fall.

Cakes won't rise.

Wine tastes metallic.

I am accidentally pregnant. We track its size from poppy seed to lentil to blueberry.

And then the barfing begins.

I have no interest in food, but if my stomach gets even close to empty, I start gagging. If I cough or sneeze, I throw up. I cannot be anywhere else except in the miserable nauseated present moment.

=

I drive all over Los Angeles teaching yoga. I float my arms up with my students, and then I fold my ever-expanding body down toward my legs. *Soften your jaw, broaden your collarbones, follow your breath, lengthen your exhale.* The only time the nausea settles is when I'm helping other people breathe.

Many evenings, just after sunset, as I start dreading the long nauseated night to come, all I want is for the baby to die.

=

At twenty weeks pregnant, my nausea lifts.

My baby will be made of cottage cheese pancakes.

=

We look at vaginal maps.

It's down at the bottom. The curvy part.

We read about massaging the perineum with almond oil to prepare for the ring of fire during crowning: the moment when the baby stretches everything down there from a quarter-size hole into a softball-size exit. But first we have to find my perineum.

Here?

No. Lower.

Here?

Ow.

I want to skip the next part.

=

When my grandmother Phyllis goes into labor with my mother in 1945, my grandfather is told to stay in the waiting room until it's all over. She puts on a gas mask and wakes up to a baby girl.

=

I drive around Los Angeles, six days overdue.

I have scrubbed the house every day for weeks. We have everything set up for a home birth. The freezer is filled with lasagnas, enchiladas, garden burgers, and chocolate chip cookies. There are no more lists to check off.

The baby kicks its legs around, curling its feet up into my lower ribs, pressing its head down.

I pull over to the side of the road.

You can stay in there.

I watch the baby push through my belly, a foot an elbow a knee gliding up, down, right, left.

You don't ever need to come out.

=

When my mom goes into labor with me in 1970, my father is tolerated in the delivery room. I am occiput posterior and I get stuck on the way out. After thirty-six hours of Lamaze-guided labor, the doctor brings out the baby-extracting device that looks like a large set of kitchen tongs you might use to retrieve a blanched peach from boiling water. These forceps press too hard on one side of my head, leaving a half-moon-shaped scar next to my right eye.

=

I stand up and tell M to turn off the movie because it feels like someone is shoving a cattle prod up into my vagina.

I'm hot. No. Wait. I'm cold.

My insides are heading out.

Why am I crying?

M lights candles and puts on our birth mix CD. I put out my arms. He draws me in and we awkwardly sway to Björk. I throw up down his back.

He turns off the music and lights more candles we've set around the living room. I throw up again. He blows out the candles. I throw up in the kitchen sink. Out the back door. I throw up so vigorously that my mucus plug pops out, a red splat on the bath mat.

My body is making room.

For twelve hours, I walk, moaning, forearms and cheek pressing the wall's cool paint, stunned by the newness of the pain, each contraction more impossible than the last.

The midwife-doula cavalry arrives at sunrise. They set up the birthing tub in the middle of the living room and halfway through filling it up we run out of hot water. M puts all our pasta pots on the stove and boils water. He is grateful to finally feel useful. They tell him where to place his hands during the next contraction, how to look into my eyes, how to pretend he's not scared.

We climb into the tub together. M surrounds me, his belly to my back, his inner thighs to my outer thighs, our arms stacked on the sides of the tub. The warm water supports my heavy belly. The pressure on my pelvic floor starts to soften.

The shades are drawn. The light is gentle. The voices are calm.

After each contraction, I collapse back into a deep, snoring nap, waking up with another woman's eyes staring into mine, just as the intensity starts to build again.

Phyllis, if you feel any urge to push, then just go for it.

After each contraction, like a buoy to the surface of the water, the baby elevators back up the birth canal to where it started.

Until finally, after three hours, it stays down and locked into position. I can feel it working just as hard as I am. It wants out.

This is when the burning begins. The ring of fire we read about. An excruciating slow-motion stretching of the perineum.

A midwife guides my hand down between my legs. I don't recognize anything down there. All is taut and ready to pop.

And then I feel it. The warmth, the hair, my crowning baby. This is all I need. I find strength behind strength, and push like a motherfucker.

Out it swims. And *bam* its eyes open and lock on mine.

Someone tells me it's a girl.

I look down at her perfect eyes and wonder why her lips are blue.

A midwife yanks my baby out of my arms and works on her for far too long, shoving tubes down her throat, placing an oxygen mask over her face, tilting her on her side to expel all the gunk her lungs collected on the way out.

I'm still wrapped in M's arms in the lukewarm bloody water. I close my eyes. In my heart, I feel her die.

A midwife helps me out of the tub and wipes the birth muck off my body. I slide down to the floor. Another midwife stabs me with a needle filled with what feels like a rush of adrenaline.

Phyllis, you are hemorrhaging. I just gave you Pitocin to stop the bleeding. Your baby is okay.

My baby is not okay.

Look at her, Phyllis. Look at her.

I can't look at her.

She is okay.

And then she is back in my arms. So warm. So soft.

The midday sun illuminates our crime scene: bloody sheets, overturned chairs, contents of birth bags strewn about.

My baby girl latches onto my breast. Colostrum coats her lips and rolls down her cheek, thick and yellow and sweet like condensed milk. We see her lungs expanding, her toes wiggling, her shoulder blades winging. She is doing it all on her own.

Oh my God, I am so hungry.

A midwife spoons vanilla bean ice cream into my mouth. Nothing has ever tasted so right.

=

A few weeks after my mom gives birth to me, she stops answering the phone. She stays in her nightgown all day long. She is twenty-four, living in a five-floor walk-up in San Francisco. For eight months, she doesn't tell anyone about the darkness she feels.

=

My baby girl is in my arms all day long, tucked into my body all night long. We wake up in a puddle of breast milk that fills our ears, coats our hair, sinks down through layers of blankets and sheets and pads. My pee smells like her pee. My breath is her breath: sweet and milky and sour. We are a cloud of life and death and ferment.

Exhale down. Inhale up. Exhale down. Inhale up. Faster and faster. Bouncing up and down on an exercise ball is the only thing that gets her to stop screaming. On each bounce I hear my brain crack into my skull and I feel my organs—already displaced from nine months of pregnancy—floating around the cavernous insides of my torso, crashing into one another.

If I put her down she screams. If I hold her she screams. Swaddling, swaying, singing aren't enough. I walk in circles around the block because I am scared to cross the street. I am scared to leave my nursing chair. I am scared I won't be able to keep her safe.

One breastfeeding session leads into the next. I use one arm to hold her to my breast. With the other arm, I grasp the side of the padded nursing chair. I can't look down because I am convinced the earth will fall out from under me.

Images pulse in my head, violent flashes in which I smash her brain in with a flashlight or throw her fragile body against the wall. Thousands of times, I watch her die.

=

We sleep through the night enough times.

I kiss her fingertips enough times.

She one-arm commando scooches on her belly from the kitchen to the living room to the bedroom enough times.

I start leaving her in the living room, walking around the corner to make coffee, believing that she will be alive when I return.

I teach yoga.

I cross the street.

Cakes rise.

=

We cover the living room floor with a tarp, strap her into her Graco Deluxe yellow-and-turquoise picnic-patterned high chair and open a dozen jars of baby food.

I watch her taste. I watch her smile. I watch her taste some more. She doesn't need me. I start to fall head over heels.

=

We move to Berkeley, in the condo above my grandmother Phyllis. We worry a lot about how noisy we are. The barking dog. Our toddler's tantrums. Our fights. My occasional throwing of a plate or a book or a clog. Every single episode of *Six Feet Under*.

=

If I hear a baby screaming in a restaurant, I have to leave the room, to shake the sadness out of my body, to blot the milk that flows from my breasts.

M and I talk about having another baby.

=

I get certified as a birth doula. It's strategic. Maybe by helping other women, I can have an easier experience the second time around. Maybe I can change the way my own body works by watching others.

I hold laboring women in cars and beds and on bathroom floors. I massage their third eyes, swollen ankles, sacra. I hold their sisters and mothers and partners. I bring them ice chips and granola bars. I help them remember their birth plans. I help them let go of their birth plans. Drugs. No drugs. *Phyllis, get me the motherfucking drugs.* I tell them they can do it. That they are doing it. I watch them dance and squat. I watch them punch pillows and partners. I watch them hum and om and grunt and yell and scream and cry their babies out. Angrily. Defiantly. Ecstatically. Quietly. I tell them that softening the jaw can help relax the pelvic floor. I see husbands so strong and focused on their laboring wives that they forget I'm even in the room. Lights are dimmed. Candles are lit. Lights are thrown back on. Baby crash carts are rolled in. I watch planned C-sections and emergency C-sections. I see babies pulled and sucked out. I see stuck placentas and torn perinea. So much blood and vomit and shit. Needles into spines. Scalp monitors. Birth after stillborn. Birth after the loss of a parent, a partner, a child. All the stories so huge.

=

In 1971, twenty-four weeks pregnant with her second child, my mother bleeds through her white tennis dress and all over the bathroom floor. To stop the contractions, the doctor recommends bed rest and shots of alcohol. My dad has to leave on a business trip so my grandmother Phyllis wakes up my groggy mother every few hours with brandy. But nothing stops the down-and-out squeezing of her uterus. Alone in the delivery room, she pushes the baby out and he dies within a few minutes. She doesn't hold him. She doesn't name him. She doesn't say goodbye.

=

I know I'm pregnant again when I find myself in the anchovy aisle, tracing my fingers along the tins, my mouth watering, my skin tingling, my body overly alive.

The headache comes first. Then the bleeding. Back to the beginning each time.

So, doctor, how are my husband's sperm?

His sperm are fine.

So what's the problem?

Your FSH is so high that I don't even think you should waste your money trying IVF with your own eggs. You are experiencing early ovarian failure. You should look into egg donors. You will keep miscarrying.

I move on to the next doctor.

When the third fertility specialist tells me that I have a 4 percent chance of bringing another baby to term, I decide to stop listening to the numbers and start listening to my body.

The monthly pounding and aching of my right ovary is called mittelschmerz. When I feel it, I know that an egg is being released.

For the first time in my life, I look down and examine my cervical fluid. It shifts throughout the cycle. Sometimes it's clear and clean-smelling. Other times it's viscous like a glue stick or stinky like colatura di alici. When it stretches out like egg whites, I know it's time.

After sex, I do precarious headstands on the bed to help the sperm move to my egg.

Another pregnancy. Another miscarriage.

I get chiropractic care, I take homeopathic remedies, I buy ovulation kits.

Four, five, six more miscarriages.

I do weekly acupuncture, I assist in a postnatal yoga class just to be near all those spiking hormones, I buy pregnancy tests in bulk.

Pregnancy number nine sticks. For two weeks, then four, then six, then eight. Like one of those Velcro balls that my four-year-old daughter throws at a dartboard, I keep expecting the baby to fall out of me onto the floor.

I press down on my belly with my fingertips. She flutters back. I name her. Willow Tassajara. A daughter do-over. This time I will love her right away. I will not want to hurt her.

I learn I'm having a boy.

=

I sit on the back porch with my daughter, pretending to smell the rosemary, the lavender, the matilija poppies. I want to scoop up the dirt and eat it. The desire is a thirst. Not a hunger. I have pica. Nothing will quench this feeling until I push my baby out.

=

I pin my four-year-old daughter down, my hands to her forearms, my forehead to hers, all sticky with sweaty, stringy bangs. *You are okay. You don't need to scream. I am here to help you.* I think she is calm so I roll off to rest. But she isn't done. She throws a chair. This time, I hold her from behind, crossing her arms to her chest. I finally feel her body soften back into my very pregnant belly. I let go. She moves to her art table. She organizes her pencils. She draws colorful squirrels and rainbows with pots of gold. Hand in hand, we drift into the kitchen. Drained. Relieved. And we prep. We review the chocolate chip cookie recipe and place all the ingredients into mixing bowls and ramekins. *Mama, I am ready.* Her meticulousness reminds me to slow down.

=

At 6:00 a.m., my daughter takes my hands. *You can do it, Mama, you can do it, you can do it, you can do it.*

At 11:00 a.m., I peer down into the toilet, searching for my baby boy in the water, thinking he has come out with a gush of fluid and blood, unaware that my water has just broken.

At noon, I head to the hospital. They ask me to sign admission forms. I can't work the pen. I can't remember my name.

From my work as a birth doula, I know this hospital well. The shortcuts. How to get a nurse's attention fast. Where to find the ice chips and the Jell-O and the extra pillows. But I don't care about any of that. I just need the pain to stop. I head right to triage.

As the nurse maneuvers her gloved hand way up inside me, I try to guess my dilation from the look on her face. I need a big number. At one, the cervix is thick and almost closed, at ten it is completely thinned out and open. I want at least an eight. She flashes a five and throws the glove into the medical-waste bin. *Fuck. A five. How is that possible?*

=

My doula places her hands on my shoulders, presses down so hard that I feel my heel bones penetrate the cold hard floor, and says, *Phyllis, this baby is about to come out.*

I have several contractions on my walk to the delivery room. Each one more of a full-body experience than the last. Unlike my daughter's birth, when the pain was isolated in the pelvic floor and belly, this time it's an inner tornado corkscrewing down through my entire torso, as if I might fly apart, limb from limb.

The doctor runs in out of breath, wearing jeans. I wonder why he doesn't take the time to change into his scrubs. He checks me.

You're at ten, Phyllis. You can push.

Three pushes and he's out.

I look down at my boy and trace his soft cheek with the back of my finger, checking to see that he is a complete baby, that he has ribs and kneecaps and shins and clavicles.

I rub his vernix into my dry elbows. I massage his arches. I trip out on his blue eyes.

I hand M our second baby.

We did it.

No, you did it.

I lie on the mess of sticky, bloody sheets and let many sets of hands try to put me back together again.

Someone shows me how to massage my uterus to help bring it down to size.

Someone washes my torn labia with a peri bottle filled with warm water.

Someone feeds me a chocolate chip cookie.

Someone sneaks my placenta out of the hospital.

=

My friends get the call. The placenta is waiting for them in my fridge. They try to hack it up. They gag. The organ is vascular and tough. My kitchen knives are dull.

But they know I am desperate. They know that it might give me back some of what I lost so quickly in childbirth: the blood, the hormones. And they know I will try anything that might help me fall in love with my baby right away. Anything to prevent the violent images from coming back. They braise my placenta with their homemade ragout until it's soft enough to eat for dinner. They stir in crème fraîche. This is a mistake. The placenta chunks stand out like sinewy beacons.

They bring placenta Bolognese straight to my hospital bed. I eat it slowly, each bite a prayer. As my son is passed from one set of arms to the next, a familiar dysphoric fog rolls in over my toes and knees and elbows, in toward my center.

I turn away. I don't want them to see what I feel.

=

I trick myself into loving him.

I say *I love you, I love you, I love you so much.* Even though I don't feel it. Even though I don't believe it. Because love must be cumulative.

This time I tell anyone who will listen. I describe the pit in my stomach. The deep sadness I feel all over my body. How I kill him over and over again in my head.

I feed him solid foods as early and as much as I can. Anything to not feel like he is part of my body. I purée stew. I mix avocados with yogurt. I mash squash and potatoes.

I take photos. Through the viewfinder, I watch him explore. I press the shutter of my camera down halfway, focusing on his eyeball. He looks up like a puppy. Those eyes. They help.

After eight months, I start to tip over into love.

=

I roll down, vertebra by vertebra, flatten my hands on the bottom of the tub, lean my weight forward into my fingertips, and exhale flip fly up into a handstand.

My screaming babies are always with me.

My feet flex back. My heels press into the tiles.

I hear their screams in washing-machine cycles, squeaky drawers, car brakes.

The water beats down on my upside-down face, burning my nose, my throat.

I hear them in the roar of a crowd, the music at a café, the chirps of the birds.

My fingers grip. My arms shake. My jaw trembles.

I hear them in the silence.

Upside down in the shower, I can almost erase them.

=

One hour down, five more to go. Berkeley to Los Angeles. I am driving far away from my son for the first time since he was born.

I start to cry.

I can't untangle the relief from the grief from the anxiety from the silence.

Because he is that kid.

The one who climbs out of a three-story window if it's open, who scales the fence to see what is on the other side, who picks up the knife just because it is sitting there, who runs out into the street and almost gets hit by a car, who sees a mushroom growing in the grass and quickly eats it.

The monotony of time and of the road feel alien. I can barely keep my eyes open. I pull off the I-5 freeway and into the Apricot Tree parking lot. I lock the doors and take a disco nap.

=

M's voice blasts through the car's Bluetooth: *It's up to you. It's up to you. It's up to you.*

I am scared that this time I won't come back. That this time I will actually harm the baby.

I get out of the car and try to peek into Planned Parenthood, cozily tucked between Jo-Ann Fabrics and Mel-O-Dee cocktail lounge, but the windows are tinted like my Volvo wagon's.

The waiting room is filled with women who all look how I feel. Nauseated, dragged down, confused, ready to run. *Harry Potter and the Goblet of Fire* flashes from a television that no one is watching, the volume set so high it makes me vibrate from sternum to sit bones. Harry is trying to murder someone without a nose. I almost throw up on the man next to me.

They bring me back and sit me down.

Do you feel safe at home?

Yes. Oh yes.

Do you want a photo of the sonogram?

I text M, *do you want a photo?*

too painful, he texts back.

I lean back on the crinkly white paper, spread my legs, and feel a condom-covered vaginal wand enter my birth canal and magically transmit the image of a six-week, two-day-old embryo onto a screen above. The beginning of another one beats loudly in my ears.

I ask for a photo.

Are you ready to pass this pregnancy?

My mouth can no longer form words, causing trapped animal sounds to escape my lips. I nod and she drops a pill into my hand that will stop the flow of progesterone needed to maintain a pregnancy.

I swallow that first pill with very little water, as if letting it slide slowly down my raw throat will allow me the freedom to change my mind. They give me four more pills to take at home the next day that will cause my thickened uterus and the embryo that's embedded in its walls to shed.

I leave the fluorescent lights of Planned Parenthood and walk through the parking lot, my lips and fingertips and toes numb, pregnancy-hormone ravenous, high on abortion drugs.

The next day, I kick M and the kids out of the house, take some Vicodin, and carefully place the four pills inside my right cheek. I'm supposed to let them sit in my mouth without swallowing for ten minutes. A chalkiness coats my tongue. I drool. I worry that too much of the drug is escaping my body and the abortion will only work halfway so I catch the liquid in a cup and swallow it back down.

I get in bed. The Vicodin makes my bones heavy and my thoughts hallucinatory. I feel hands shoveling my insides out. I imagine what this baby would have looked like, smelled like, how deeply I might have been able to love it.

I wake up and stumble into the kitchen. I sit in the hot sun on my back porch and eat ice cream.

All I feel is the cold, custardy sweetness sliding over my tongue and down my throat.

=

After too many falls and too many hips broken, my grandmother Phyllis can no longer live downstairs from us in Berkeley. I visit her often in her assisted living apartment in San Francisco, nine floors up, sealed in silence above the swirling Van Ness Avenue. Even when it's foggy, the light slices through the living room windows. There are no dust bunnies. The kitchen is empty. Her bed is always made.

How are you doing, Grandma?

I miss all of your noise.

=

I grasp my hands together. I want to throw something out the window. A phone. A set of keys.

M stops the car. I grab my purse, slam the door, and cross the street. I internally rant *I don't want this, I don't want this, I don't want this,* flapping my arms like a distressed Italian mama from Fellini's *La Strada*.

I sit down on the corner and hold my head in my hands. I force my mouth closed. I am working on my temper.

M turns the car around and parks across the street. He crosses in my direction but stays far enough away to let me know he doesn't like me yet. That he's not ready to move on. He's not here to make things better. We start yelling.

The children watch from the car. They pound on the window. I read their little lips as they repeat over and over again, *stop fighting, stop fighting, stop fighting.* Their big tears fall.

Our words do not land. They miss each other entirely. They are predictable, they are loaded, they are twenty-five-years layered and bound.

And then there's nothing more to yell. And we're still on the corner. And it's dinnertime.

We agree we must get in the car. We agree the neighbors don't need to watch us fight. We agree it is now too much for our children to bear.

He slips into the driver's seat. I slip into the passenger seat, breathing as if I've just run ten times around the block.

Mom. Dad. You know what you have to do?

What?

All you have to do is say you're sorry. That's it. That's what you've taught us. Come on, Mom. Say it.

Exactly. It's that simple, adds my daughter. *But say it like you mean it.*

Our son crawls up to the front seat and settles in my lap. He pulls my right arm as if it's a seat belt, extending it across my body toward M. He takes M's wrist and yanks. As hard as he pulls, my son is not strong enough to make us touch.

We all take our arms back.

We sit in silence.

Say it, Mom. Tell Dad you're sorry.

I'm sorry.

Dad? Say it.

I'm sorry.

We are good actors.

Our daughter goes back to her iPod. Our son resumes his nonstop narration of the world.

Awww. I saw a cat. I love cats. Can we get one? Please? Can I have some gum? That tree is so tall. Wow. Mom. Dad. Look. It climbs up to the sky. And then you can step onto the clouds if you want. Can you sit on a cloud? Mom. Mom. Mom. Can you sit on a cloud?

You can't sit on a cloud.

Please, Mom?

Some things, I can't control.

M and I fake it through dinner. Through bedtime routine. We fall asleep honoring the invisible line that divides our king-size bed into separate sleeping capsules. We wake up and fake it through lunch-making, shoe-finding, tooth-brushing, drop-off.

Until I can't bear it anymore. I ask M the question I've asked almost every night for twenty-five years. *What do you want for dinner?*

I want some stew. And I want to drink some intense red wine with you.

The meat cooks all day, the smell gets sucked into the wall-to-wall carpeting, the sofa, the winter coats. Meat is under my fingernails. Fat drippings speckle my boots.

We fill warm corn tortillas with the spicy meat, cabbage salad, avocado halves, jalapeño pickles. We splash it all with crème fraîche.

=

As I turn off my daughter's lights and tuck in her sprawling legs, I get a whiff of her sweetness. I slip into her bed, press my lips to her temple, and hold her clammy hands. She feels so half-baked, her bones so close to the surface.

I look in my son's room. He is snoring and sweating, skin all second-grade shellacked with dirt and sweat.

I check on M. Awake. I put on the lingerie I got on sale at Target.

Have you seen my vibrator?

I am not your vibrator's keeper.

The dog scratches on the door. I let him in.

I turn off the lights and slide back into bed. The dog scratches to go out. I let him out. I get back in bed. I turn to M. Everything is in place.

M turns on the light. *I need to put the laundry in the dryer. And why are you wearing that thing, my love? I really want to see your body. I'll be right back.*

I close my eyes. I ache with fatigue. My ankles throb. I don't want to explain anything. How sometimes I don't want to be seen.

I hear M locking the front door, filling the dog's water bowl, flipping the laundry.

Mom! Mom! Mom! Mooooooooooooooooooooooooooom!

I jump up, put on my bathrobe, and run out into the hall. There stands my daughter. I know what she is about to say.

We make it to the bathroom just in time. I pull her hair back. I hold my breath until it's all over.

I guide her to our bed. She sleeps between us, my hand resting on her chest, my mind surfing the rise and fall of my twelve-year-old's breath until the sun comes up.

=

My grandmother Phyllis lies in a hospital bed, staring at the ceiling, hands wrapped around the club-shaped necklace that hangs from a heavy silver chain around her neck. Fifty years before, my grandfather soldered these three coins together.

I blow her a kiss. She drops the necklace and extends her arms. I sink into her fragile chest.

Grandma, how are you? What do you need? Are you hungry? Are you craving anything?

I am craving you.

I sit next to the bed and hold her hand. She closes her

eyes and her mouth falls slack, causing her to look simultaneously young and old. I want to try her body on like a coat. To wear her ninety-three years.

I close my eyes and see her in the kitchen scraping all the tuna out of the can and then *whack whack whacking* a big spoonful of Best Foods mayonnaise on the side of the bowl. I watch her chop the celery, the knife bouncing dangerously close to her fingertips. She cuts the green onions with scissors, adds a squeeze of lemon, and then a slow sprinkling of salt and a few turns of pepper. A thorough stir. I see her lean in and give it all a calm and steady stare. She rarely tastes. She just knows when it is right. She scoops the tuna salad onto toasted bread, places another piece of toast on top, and cuts it on the diagonal. Onto the tray with Fritos, a bottle of white wine, two glasses. *You will join me for a glass of wine, won't you?*

The nurse places dinner in front of my grandmother. Our eyes open.

Tell me, Grandma. How was the emergency room today? You must be exhausted. I'm glad they released you.

They told me I only weigh 108 pounds.

I haven't weighed 108 pounds since I was fourteen. How about you, Grandma?

I was 108 pounds before I started this glorious string of people.

She moves her arms open as if acknowledging generations, as if I'm not the only one in the room.

=

I move my hand over the dough's smooth surface, smiling when I see the chunks of butter.

Damn, you are so beautiful.

My son calls out from another room, *Who the heck are you talking to, Mom?*

I yell, *I am talking to my tart dough!*

He yells back, *Mom, I've been spending a lot of time thinking about numbers and how they go on and on and on without ever ending.*

I find him. He is in the living room. In a ball. On the sofa. Sunburn splashed across his cheeks like war paint.

He unfurls his warm limbs, pulls me in, and squeezes my upper body until I yell at him to stop. I stack his body on top of mine. We compare leg length, arm length, tooth length.

I feel the fidget that travels through his system like an electrical impulse. I wonder how he ever turns it off.

How is forever even possible, Mom?

I massage my way up his spine, our hearts punching beats back and forth, until his limbs drop down, all looseness and lead.

I slip out and make a strawberry balsamic tart.

=

My grandmother places her napkin in her lap and starts nibbling on a chicken wing.

Grandma, what do you want for your birthday dinner?

I keep thinking about your tarts. I love tarts. I want tarts.

Oh, God, me too.

And those avocado bowls you make.

What about dessert?

We smile. It must be chocolate.

=

My son stumbles into the kitchen.

How was your nap?

What nap, Mom? I didn't sleep at all. I was just resting my eyes. I haven't taken a nap since I was two.

I slide over some scraps of dough.

Come on over. Make a mini pie.

I watch. He rolls it out gently, adding a sprinkle of flour to prevent sticking, a quick flip, a bit more flour.

He overfills the pocket with a spoonful of Nutella, a squeeze of honey, a large strawberry. As I open the oven door, he yells out, *Wait, one more thing.* He tops his pie with a pretzel. *Yes, Mom, now it's perfect.*

=

My grandmother Phyllis gets out of bed and starts putting on her shoes.

You know we're not going to celebrate your birthday for a few more weeks, right?

She pauses. She nods. She continues getting dressed.

I help her put on a sweater. She sighs and stares straight ahead. Her hair all two-year-old-rat's-nest puffed out in the back.

Grandma, do you have a brush?

They took it away from me.

I find it under a pile of *New Yorker* magazines.

I might have some lipstick. Do you want some?

Yes, they took that away too.

I hand her a mirror and my darkest lipstick. She applies lipstick as gracefully as she cooks.

Grandma, do you miss cooking?

Yes.

What do you miss about it?

Absolutely everything.

＝

Phyllis, it's Mom.

The voicemail comes in right after I leave the grocery store. It's a Monday in January. Martin Luther King Day. No school. The kids are in the back seat. We listen through the car's Bluetooth.

Call me please.

I hear death in her voice.

=

I pull out my grandmother Phyllis's KitchenAid mixer, a wedding gift from 1943. I never think it's going to work. It is lighter and squatter than the modern ones, and there's always a trail of grease dripping down the side.

I cream the butter and sugar on medium speed. My daughter pours in shiny hazelnut butter. We turn the mixer up to full speed and beat the batter until it glides up the sides of the bowl and fills with air. She slowly scrapes down the sides and adds an egg. I add another egg and too much vanilla. We fold in the sifted dry ingredients. Flour flies up and makes me sneeze. Seven times. Like it always does.

=

I step out onto my back porch with my coffee. Berkeley smells like it's wearing too much jasmine perfume. A severe drought has brought early blossoms. Mother Nature is confused. The morning light brings my details into relief: the bloody gash on my shin from walking into my son's bike in the middle of the night, the dog hair on my black dress, the olive oil stains on my leggings.

I say to my herbs, *I am getting so fucking old.* Again with a smile: *I am getting so fucking old.* That's better.

I ask my lemon tree if it's ready to die. I have forgotten to water, feed, talk to it for over twelve years. It doesn't produce lemons—it struggles out gnarled bitter green balls.

I rush back into the kitchen—sloshing coffee down my front—to remove the pizza from the oven, line up the lunch tins, peel the carrots.

Come here for a second.

M's voice has nothing in it. No resentment. No needs. No frustration. No anger.

I walk over and place my hands on his shoulders. He pulls me in, hands cupping my ass.

I say *more* with my arms, pelvis, sighs.

He says *not now, no time* by releasing his arms.

I de-lint my daughter's jacket, tie my son's shoes, kiss my husband with my stinky coffee breath, and yell them all out the door.

I brush my teeth, put on a bra, and saw down the lemon tree.

＝

RECIPES

=

TART DOUGH

makes enough for one 8- or 9-inch tart or galette;

double the recipe for a pie

I use this recipe for all my sweet and savory pies, tarts, and galettes.

If you have time, make the dough a day ahead so that it can chill in the refrigerator overnight. If you are in a hurry, you can chill it in the freezer for 2 hours before you roll it out.

If there are any kids around, give them the dough scraps. Let them overknead and over-roll and oversmush it into mini tarts. Then they can fill the dough–lined tart molds with honey or berries or chocolate chips.

½ cup water

½ cup (1 stick) unsalted butter, right out of the fridge

1¼ cups all-purpose flour

¾ teaspoon kosher salt

Put the water in a small pitcher with a handful of ice cubes.

Cut the butter into ½-inch cubes.

In a large mixing bowl, whisk together the flour and salt.

Place half the chilled butter cubes into the flour mixture. With your fingertips, cut the butter into the flour until the mixture resembles coarse cornmeal. Just keep squeezing the chunks of butter between your fingertips, almost like you're trying to snap with all your fingers at once.

Add the remaining butter and continue using your fingertips to incorporate until the chunks from the second batch of butter are about the size of peas (they'll be larger than the first round). Add a few tablespoons of the cold water and gently mix it in with a fork. Add another tablespoon of the water, mixing with the fork and jostling the bowl. Add more as needed, 1 tablespoon at a time. It's ready when there are still some dry pockets but the dough is just starting to gather into about 1-inch globules. It will still be quite loose, so don't expect it to come together yet into a dough. You will be pressing it into a disc in a moment.

Spread out an 18-inch length of plastic wrap. Empty the contents of the bowl into the middle of the plastic wrap. Fold up the sides of the plastic wrap to press the dough into a round or square disc (depending on the shape of your tart). After about 15 seconds of pressing and molding, it should come together to form a delicate mass. Remember, you aren't kneading it, just bringing it together. You should still be able to see small pea-size chunks of butter. Wrap tightly and refrigerate overnight or for at least 6 hours or freeze for 2 hours before rolling out.

Before rolling out the dough, let it stand at room temperature until slightly softened, about 20 to 30 minutes depending on the temperature of your kitchen.

TARTE TATIN

serves 6 to 8

For this recipe, you will need a 12-inch ovenproof cast-iron skillet (a 10-inch will work if that's all you have; just roll the dough out to 12 inches instead of 14 inches). Clean the heck out of it if it has been used for meat or fish. I scrub my skillet with salt and half a lemon and then boil water in it for ten minutes.

Ideally, you want to use apples that will keep their shape when cooked. There are many varieties that will work. I usually use Braeburn, Gala, or Fuji.

You can use homemade (page 181) or store-bought tart dough, but puff pastry is my favorite. I don't make my own puff pastry because life is too short. I buy Dufour.

1 (14-ounce) sheet puff pastry

5 to 8 apples (about 3 pounds)

½ cup granulated sugar

2 tablespoons unsalted butter

1 tablespoon vanilla extract or vanilla bean crush (vanilla extract with seeds, which can be ordered easily online)

2 teaspoons lemon juice

1 teaspoon lemon zest

¼ teaspoon kosher salt

Take the puff pastry out of the freezer and let it thaw enough so that it's easy to roll out. This can take anywhere from 30 to 60 minutes depending on the temperature of your kitchen.

Preheat the oven to 375°F.

On a lightly floured surface, roll out the puff pastry into a 14-by-14-inch square (about ⅛-inch thick). With a pizza cutter, cut off the corners so you're left with a circle that's 14 inches in diameter (save the scraps in the freezer and drape them over some fruit for an easy cobbler). Quickly roll the puff pastry up onto your rolling pin and then roll it out onto a large plate that will fit in the fridge. Refrigerate until you're ready for assembly.

Slice the tiniest bit off both the stem and blossom ends of each apple (you will waste a tiny bit of apple but it will be so much easier to peel because the peeler will have something to grab on to). Cut each apple in half from north to south. Peel. To core, stand up an apple half with the core side facing you. Using a sharp paring knife, cut at a triangular angle, capturing the stem from top to bottom. Use a melon baller or paring knife to carefully scoop out any remaining core. As you finish coring each apple half, place it cored-side up in your skillet to see how many more you need. Tuck them in nice and tight because they will shrink while cooking. If they aren't fitting snugly enough, you can cut up an extra apple and tuck in the pieces. Transfer the apples to a plate while you cook the caramel. They will brown a bit, but don't worry, because soon enough they will be bubbling in the caramel.

Put the sugar and 2 tablespoons of water into your cast-iron pan. Stir with a wooden spoon to make sure it cooks evenly. It will start to bubble. Then it will start to darken in color and even smoke. Be brave with the color. A dark caramel tastes better and looks prettier. If you get nervous that it's caramelizing too quickly, you can lower the heat or turn it off completely—the sugar will continue to darken in the hot skillet. Just before the desired color is reached (I like the amber darkness of grade B maple syrup), turn off the heat and stir in the butter. Once the butter has melted, stir in the vanilla, lemon juice and zest, and salt.

Place the apples in the skillet on top of the caramel, cored-sides up. Simmer over low heat. This is a very important step; if you skip it, there will be too much liquid around the apples and when you flip the tarte tatin out of the pan, the hot juices will splash everywhere. Every few minutes, tilt the pan, scoop up some caramel with a heatproof spoon, and drizzle it over the apples. Once the caramel has thickened, turn off the heat. Moving quickly and carefully, place the chilled puff pastry over the apples. It will soften right away from the heat. With the back of a spoon or a dull butter knife, carefully nudge the puff pastry down the interior sides of the pan, sort of like you're tucking in a shirt. Remember that this will be the bottom of the tarte tatin and what you're pressing in will become the edge that wraps up a bit around the apples (similar to the crust of a pizza). You want it to look rustic, so don't try to make it perfect.

Bake for 30 to 35 minutes. It's done when the puff pastry is brown and firm to the touch and you can see the caramel bubbling up along the edges of the skillet.

Allow the tart to cool in the skillet for about an hour. The caramel will still be hot, so follow these instructions carefully: Run a paring knife around the edge to loosen any crust or apples stuck to the sides. Use oven mitts that cover your wrists. Place a plate that's at least 2 inches larger than the tarte tatin on top of the pan, then quickly flip it over so the crust is down and the apples are up. If some of the apples stick, use a metal spatula to lift up the stragglers and nestle them back in with the others. Make the apples glisten by using a pastry brush to paint any remaining caramel over the tops of the apples. Serve warm with crème fraîche or vanilla bean ice cream. This tarte is also super tasty served with blue or goat cheese. It doesn't freeze very well so eat any leftovers for breakfast.

CRÈME FRAÎCHE

I splash this over pasta, stews, avocado toasts, and tacos. I mix it into green goddess dressing and Pesto (page 195). It is a wonderful replacement for sour cream. I put it in my Cottage Cheese Pancakes (page 231). It's a lovely way to cut the sweet intensity of a cake or pie. Once you have it in your life, you will be tempted to use it every single day.

1 cup heavy cream
2 tablespoons buttermilk

Pour the heavy cream and the buttermilk into a jar with an available lid. Stir just to mix. Put on the lid. Leave it on the counter. The thickening and souring take anywhere from 1 to 4 days. The hotter your kitchen, the faster it will go. Stir and taste every 12 hours or so. Once it's to your liking, store it covered in the fridge for up to a month. I make this every two weeks. Every six months or so, a batch doesn't work. If it smells or tastes like blue cheese, toss it and start over.

BALSAMIC REDUCTION

Buy an inexpensive bottle of balsamic, one that contains at least 8 ounces of vinegar. (You will be reducing it by a little over half, so you want enough to yield at least ½ cup.) Pour the vinegar into a pot. Reserve the bottle. Note the height of the vinegar in the pot.

Open a window. Turn on the fan. Place the pot over high heat until the vinegar boils. Turn the heat down to medium low—just low enough so that the vinegar is simmering. Keep simmering until the vinegar has reduced a bit more than halfway. (It won't be thickened yet. Don't worry. It will thicken up as it cools.) How long it takes to reduce depends on how much vinegar you're reducing and the size of your pot. Every batch is different. Every bottle of vinegar is different.

Once reduced, turn off the heat and let cool to room temperature, about 20 to 30 minutes. Once it's cooled, if you find that it isn't quite as drizzle-worthy as you'd like, reduce it for a few more minutes. Using a funnel, pour the cooled vinegar back into the bottle. Store as you would regular vinegar. Use as you would a more special balsamic—for drizzling over salads, tarts, pastas, or open-faced sandwiches.

A few notes of caution: Your kitchen will become a balsamic vinegar steam room. Some people (like me) love the smell. It makes me feel safe. And happy. But it makes my husband feel nauseated. It can also tickle your nose. And your eyes. It made my recipe tester's cat sneeze!

JAMMY TOMATO ANCHOVY SAUCE

makes about 2½ cups

This is not an ordinary, pour-from-the-jar sauce. This is a far more versatile, concentrated sauce base that I love to use in a zillion applications (see pages 193–94). I cook the tomatoes down for several hours, until they reduce by about half, resulting in a jam-like consistency. This is especially satisfying to make in the middle of winter when good tomatoes are nowhere to be found.

Two 28-ounce cans of diced or crushed tomatoes, preferably San Marzano, with their juices

½ cup red wine

5 oil-packed anchovy fillets

3 cloves garlic, peeled and microplaned

3 tablespoons extra-virgin olive oil

2 tablespoons balsamic reduction, homemade (page 190) or store-bought aged and thick balsamic

1 tablespoon packed light or dark brown sugar

1 teaspoon lemon zest

2 teaspoons sherry or white wine vinegar

3 sprigs thyme

1 teaspoon salt

A few turns of black pepper

Pinch of Aleppo or red pepper flakes

Place all the ingredients in a large pot. Stir. Bring to a boil. Turn down the heat as low as possible to maintain a very gentle simmer. Cook for 2 to 3 hours, preferably until nearly all the liquid has evaporated and the tomatoes have the consistency of a loose jam or a dense applesauce. Stir every 20 minutes or so to make sure the tomatoes don't scorch. If the sauce base thickens too quickly or seems to be getting dry, add a bit of olive oil, wine, or water. The longer you let it simmer, the more intense it will taste. Remove the thyme sprigs. Season to taste. Depending on how chunky a texture you like, purée half or all the sauce with a hand blender or in a food processor. Store in the fridge for up to 5 days. Or freeze for up to 6 months.

A few things to do with this jammy goodness:

Dinner for 4

Cook 1 pound of pasta in salted water until al dente. Reserve a large mugful of pasta water. Drain the pasta. Coat the pasta with 1 cup (or more) of Jammy Tomato Anchovy Sauce and as much pasta water as you need to loosen up the sauce and generously coat the noodles (start with ½ mug and keep adding). Put the remaining pasta water in a pitcher on the table. Serve this dish with any of the following toppings: pine nuts, chopped parsley, goat cheese, Parmesan, olive oil, balsamic reduction, bread crumbs, coarse salt, capers, or olives.

Lunch for 1

Grill or toast some bread. Rub a peeled garlic clove all over the warm bread (it will disappear into the bread). Spread the bread generously with warm Jammy Tomato Anchovy Sauce. Top with an egg (poached or fried), a splash of olive oil, lemon zest, and coarse salt.

As a base for a pizza

Spread the sauce over pizza dough and then top with slices of mozzarella and anchovy fillets. The moment you take the pizza out of the oven, top with a generous handful of baby arugula, a few splashes of olive oil, balsamic reduction, and toasted pine nuts.

As a condiment

Use on a sandwich instead of chutney or ketchup.

PESTO

makes about 1½ cups

My pesto isn't traditional. I sometimes call it California Pesto just to keep the purists off my back. Some thoughts in no particular order:

Since pesto is often an empty-out-the-fridge/freezer endeavor, it's really important that you taste every component going in. A few rancid nuts can ruin the whole batch.

If you can, toast the nuts right before you make the pesto because they will melt the cheese, and just-made warm pesto is heavenly smeared on toast.

I use any nut I can find. (I always keep mine in my freezer so they don't go bad so quickly.) A few I love: pistachios, hazelnuts, cashews, blanched almonds, pine nuts, walnuts, and pecans.

Don't use an herbaceous or floral or bitter olive oil. Stay neutral.

Mix your acids but keep them mellow: white, Champagne, red wine, and sherry wine vinegars are my favorites. Use lemon and lime juice and zest. Stay away from orange juice because it can get funky after a few days. And while I love apple cider, rice wine, and balsamic vinegars for salad dressing, I don't use them in my pesto.

For umami depth, add some kind of fishy something: an-chovies, fish sauce, or colatura di alici. No one will know.

For greens, almost anything goes. Start with several cups of softer greens like parsley, cilantro, chives, basil, arugula, spinach. If you have tarragon or marjoram, use them in small amounts. You can bulk the pesto up with carrot or beet greens but beware of their bitterness; sometimes they are best blanched, shocked, and then squeezed almost dry before adding. The most important thing is to taste ahead of time the greens you are thinking of using.

All cheeses work. Wait. Maybe not blue cheese. But yes to Parmesan, Pecorino Romano, Piave, Asiago, Manchego, creamy or aged goat. Occasionally, I even throw in a few scraps of cheddar or Monterey Jack.

If you have the time, use a mortar and pestle. It's good ex-ercise. And it can be meditative. Start by making a paste out of the garlic and salt. Then slowly add the herbs. Then the nuts. Then cheese. Then liquefy with the olive oil. The texture and the flavor of this slower method will be different. Most of the time, I throw everything into the food processor and turn it on full throttle. Take care of yourself. It's good both ways.

Maybe add a knob of butter at the end like Marcella Hazan?

Work with what you have. Add ingredients that you love. Blop it on lamb chops. Mix it with yogurt for a slow-cooked salmon topping. Smear it on crackers. Mix it into farro or mashed potatoes or polenta or brown rice. Put it on pizza before it's baked or after. Teach your kids how to make it. Below is a template, but I have to admit I have never made it the same way twice.

> ¾ cup nuts (any combination of pine nuts, almonds, walnuts, hazelnuts, pecans, or pistachios)
>
> 2 oil-packed anchovy fillets
>
> 3 cloves garlic, peeled
>
> 8 to 10 cups loosely packed greens like basil, parsley, cilantro, and arugula (mixing tastes great)
>
> 1 teaspoon lemon zest
>
> 2 teaspoons sherry wine vinegar
>
> 1 tablespoon lemon juice
>
> ½ to 1 teaspoon kosher salt
>
> ¾ to 1 cup extra-virgin olive oil
>
> ¾ cup grated Parmesan
>
> ¼ cup fresh creamy goat cheese

Toast the nuts in a heavy-bottomed pan over medium heat, tossing every 30 seconds or so, until they just start to brown. Place the warm nuts and the rest of the ingredients in a food processor. Blitz the hell out of everything for 30 seconds. Scrape down the sides. Blitz again for

10 seconds. Taste. Too herbaceous? Add more nuts. Too bland? Add more garlic and salt. Too oily? Add more goat cheese. Adjust accordingly. Store the pesto in a jar. Top with a thin layer of olive oil to prevent browning.

The pesto lasts in the fridge for about a week. You can freeze it. Thaw it. Refreeze it. It's quite hearty and acidic and resilient.

JALAPEÑO QUICK PICKLES

makes a little over a cup

If you prefer a milder pickle, use Fresno chile peppers for medium heat or banana peppers for no heat at all. You can use this brine to pickle anything: red onions, cauliflower, cucumbers, carrots, shallots, radishes. The crunchier the vegetable, the more time you will want to cook them in the brine. Just keep tasting. Remember that they will continue to cook as they cool in the brine.

If you are using a spicy chile, wear disposable gloves. Trust me. I have spent many miserable hours trying to put out the fire on my hands. Milk, cream, olive oil, ice: nothing works! Once, I even wiped my eyes and suffered for about 24 hours. Not worth it.

Use any good-quality vinegar (except balsamic). Please don't use the bulk white kind that kills your bathroom mold.

You can liven up the brine with anything you like: thyme, rosemary, peppercorns, Aleppo pepper flakes, juniper berries.

Once the jalapeños hit the vinegar, their color will shift from a beautiful vibrant green to a dulled brownish green. Fresno chiles stay a vibrant beautiful red.

Like many things in the kitchen, pickles are always better the next day.

6 jalapeños (or about a cup of any other pickling item)

1 cup Champagne or white wine vinegar

2 teaspoons white sugar

1 teaspoon kosher salt

Put on your gloves. Slice the peppers into ⅛-inch-thick circles. To do this, hold the jalapeño at the stem end and slice starting from the small point at the tip, making your way all the way up to the stem. Set aside.

In a saucepan, combine the vinegar, sugar, and salt. Bring to a boil. Turn down the heat to low. Stir until the sugar and salt are dissolved. Add the jalapeños and simmer for two minutes. Pour into a jar. Cool. Store in the fridge for up to a month. Use the brine in salad dressings, pasta sauces, soups, and stews.

AVOCADO BOWLS WITH GARLIC ANCHOVY VINAIGRETTE

serves 6

I serve these by themselves or on top of a butter lettuce, hearts of romaine, or cabbage salad.

6 oil-packed anchovy fillets

2 large cloves garlic, peeled and microplaned or very finely chopped

2 tablespoons sherry wine vinegar

1 shallot, chopped (about 2 tablespoons)

1 tablespoon Dijon mustard

4 tablespoons extra-virgin olive oil

3 avocados

1 teaspoon coarse salt

Handful of parsley and cilantro leaves, chopped coarsely

For the vinaigrette

Heat a small heavy-bottomed pan (I use cast iron) over medium heat. Add the anchovies and a splash of their oil. Use a spatula or wooden spoon to help them disintegrate. Turn the heat to low and add the garlic. Cook for about 30 seconds until the garlic smells sweet and fragrant. Whisk in the vinegar. Once simmering, add the shallots and cook for 20 seconds. Take off the heat. Whisk in the mustard. Slowly whisk in the olive oil. Taste. Add more olive oil if it's too tangy. If it doesn't emulsify right away, sometimes it's helpful to pour it into a jar and shake vigorously.

For the avocado bowls

Halve and pit the avocados. Carefully peel off the skin. Place the halves cut-side up. Sprinkle with coarse salt. Spoon a tablespoon of the vinaigrette into each half. Top with chopped herbs.

CARAMELIZED ONION TART WITH ANCHOVIES AND OLIVES (PISSALADIÈRE)

serves 6 to 8

This was the first savory tart I ever made back when I was teaching myself to cook. I learned how to make caramelized onions from Richard Olney's book Lulu's Provençal Table. *He writes that Lulu Peyraud was very strict about how you're never supposed to brown the onions. And while I usually don't like anyone telling me that there is only one way to do something in the kitchen, I have always respected Lulu's wishes. Be prepared: they take at least an hour. Sometimes a bit more. But the reward is a sweet, golden, compote-like onion jam.*

I love eating this tart with a crisp green salad and Avocado Bowls (page 201).

This recipe makes enough onions for one 8-inch tart plus another jarful of caramelized onions to freeze or keep in the fridge to add to pastas, sandwiches, potato salads, or vinaigrettes. It's a lot of trouble, so it's nice to have some extra.

Warning: *Don't use red onions. They taste great, but the dark reddish-brown color is very unappealing.*

1 recipe Tart Dough (page 181)
5 medium yellow onions

1 tablespoon extra-virgin olive oil

1 tablespoon unsalted butter

¾ teaspoon kosher salt

Two 3-inch sprigs thyme

1 tablespoon Dijon mustard (creamy Grey Poupon is my favorite)

8 to 10 oil-packed anchovy fillets

⅓ cup Niçoise olives

Cut the onions in half from stem to root end, peel, and thinly slice. Don't be perfect about it. Discard any tough root ends. Alternatively (saving time and tears), you can use the slicing disc on your food processor to slice peeled, quartered onions.

Heat a large heavy-bottomed pan (with an available lid) over medium-high heat. Add the olive oil and butter.

Once the butter is melted, add the onions. Stir. Add the salt and thyme. Keep stirring every few minutes. The onions will give off about a ¼ cup of liquid almost immediately. When the onions have softened a bit and are starting to turn translucent (about 5 minutes), turn down the heat to low and throw on the lid. Cook, covered, stirring every 10 minutes or so, until the onions have turned very soft, translucent, and very sweet, and have released a good cup or two of juices, at least one hour and up to two. If the onions start to brown, add a splash of water or chicken stock.

Remove the lid for good, turn the heat to medium-high, and bring to a gentle boil. Cook, stirring almost constantly, until nearly all the liquid in the pan has evaporated and the onions have taken on a marmalade-like consistency (golden yellow, honey-sweet, and still moist), about 15 minutes. Stay with it. Don't let it burn. Stir, stir, stir.

Locate the thyme sprigs and discard. Taste. Add salt if needed. Cool. The onions keep in a covered container for a few days in the fridge and for several months in the freezer.

Take your tart dough out of the fridge or freezer. Once it's soft enough to roll out, preheat the oven to 350°F. Roll out your tart dough until it's about 10 inches in diameter and ⅛-inch thick. Press into an 8- or 9-inch tart pan. You can also do this as a free-form tart. Thinly spread the mustard over the bottom of the tart shell with a pastry brush or a butter knife. Spread at least a cup of the cooked onions over the bottom of the prepared tart shell. Top with lots of anchovies and olives in any pattern that you like. Bake until the crust is just set and the onions are golden brown, about 35 to 40 minutes. Serve warm or at room temperature with a crisp green salad. Freezes beautifully.

BRAISED CHICKEN

serves 4

When I want roast chicken, I go to my parents' house. It just tastes better when they make it. In my kitchen, I usually braise it. Mostly because I am a bit of a wimp when it comes to cooking meat. And I am less likely to overcook chicken if I slowly simmer it in liquid.

Before making this dish, I search the back of my fridge for forgotten olives, capers, jalapeño pickle brine, and old wine. I save red wine from the end of dinner that I find in glasses and keep it in a mason jar in the fridge and use it for braises and stews (it cooks for a long time so no need to be grossed out!).

Serve the tender chicken and the briny broth over a mound of creamy polenta, farro, mashed potatoes, or brown rice.

4 whole chicken legs (leg and thigh combo)

1 lime

2 teaspoons kosher salt

1 teaspoon crushed Aleppo, Marash, or red pepper flakes

1 tablespoon vegetable oil

1 tablespoon extra-virgin olive oil

½ red onion, diced (about ½ cup)

4 cloves garlic, microplaned, pressed, or chopped

2 oil-packed anchovy fillets

Three 2-inch sprigs thyme

1 cup red wine

1 cup canned chopped tomatoes (or the same amount of chopped
and very ripe fresh tomatoes)

½ cup random olives from the back of your fridge, any combination works and pits are fine (just warn the eaters)

1 tablespoon capers, plus their brine

2 tablespoons jalapeño pickle brine (see page 199), optional

¼ cup chopped parsley for garnish

Zest of 1 lemon for garnish

Squeeze lime juice all over the chicken pieces. Season both
sides of each piece with kosher salt and pepper flakes. Go
do something else for a bit.

After about 30 minutes, put an ovenproof heavy-bottomed
pot (with an available lid) over medium heat. Preheat the
oven to 350°F. Add the vegetable oil. Once it's shimmering, use tongs to carefully lower each leg skin-side down
into the pot (if they don't fit, do this in two batches or
else they will steam instead of brown). You want them
sizzling and moving toward a nice deep dark brown color.
This takes 6 to 8 minutes. Turn the pieces over and brown
the other sides. With the tongs, transfer the chicken legs
to a plate. Pour all but a thin slick of the grease out of the
pot, leaving behind the brown bits.

Turn down the heat to low under your pot. Add the olive oil and onion. Use a wooden spoon to scrape the goodies off the bottom of the pot and incorporate into the onion. Cook the onion, stirring occasionally, until it just starts to soften, about 5 minutes. Add the garlic and the anchovy fillets. Turn up the heat to medium. Stir for 30 seconds until the mixture starts to smell nutty, fishy, and sweet. Pour in the wine, tomatoes, olives, pickle brine, thyme, and capers. Stir and bring to a boil. Turn off the heat and place the browned chicken back in skin-side down. You want the liquid to come halfway up the sides of the chicken but not completely submerge it. Add chicken stock or wine if necessary. Turn off the heat. Place the pot in the oven with the lid on. After 20 minutes, turn the chicken pieces over, skin-side up. Leave the lid off and cook for another 20 minutes. Check the chicken. You want it tender and just starting to pull away from the bone. But don't stress. The beauty of braised chicken is that it's hard to overcook.

Slide the pot to the back of your stove for a few hours. Or, once cool, refrigerate for up to 3 days. This dish gets better with time. When you're ready to eat, use tongs to take the chicken out of the sauce and place the pieces on a plate. Heat the sauce back up. Taste it and adjust. It might need salt or a splash of sherry wine vinegar. Put the chicken back in the sauce. Reheat over low temperature on the stovetop or in the oven. Garnish with chopped parsley and lemon zest.

SPICY BEEF STEW

safely serves 4-ish with some leftovers

The roots of this recipe come from a short rib nacho recipe written by Melissa Clark in The New York Times.

The spices used are the ones that many of us have on hand, that have been sitting in our cupboards forever. My paprika was a gift from a friend who went to Hungary. I always have ground cinnamon for my Christmas gingerbread. And I bought some chipotle chili years ago to make chili. And now that I have one of those high-velocity turbo blenders, it makes me so happy to use a random bottle of beer from the back of my fridge and wilty cilantro (stems and all) as I move toward less waste in the kitchen.

Very important note: *This stew is not meant to be eaten by itself. It needs friends and toppings like cabbage salad with Garlic Anchovy Vinaigrette (page 201), Avocado Bowls (page 201), Crème Fraîche (page 189), Jalapeño Quick Pickles (page 199), and warm tortillas.*

> 2 pounds beef chuck stew meat, cut into 1½- to 2-inch cubes
>
> Freshly ground black pepper and kosher salt
>
> 1 cup amber ale (or any beer you have lying around)
>
> 1 cup canned tomatoes, diced or whole

4 oil-packed anchovy fillets

4 cloves garlic

1 tablespoon tomato paste

1 jalapeño, stemmed, halved, and seeded (for more fire, use the
   seeds)

1 bunch parsley (half for stewing liquid, half for garnish)

1 bunch cilantro (half for stewing liquid, half for garnish)

1 teaspoon hot or sweet smoked paprika (or a combination)

1 teaspoon chili powder (chipotle if you can find it)

1 teaspoon cinnamon

2 tablespoons vegetable oil, for browning the meat

1 tablespoon extra-virgin olive oil

1 yellow onion, peeled and diced

1 lime

Sherry wine vinegar, optional

Generously season the stew meat all over with salt and pepper.

Preheat the oven to 300°F. Adjust your oven racks so that your pot fits on the middle rack. I use a sturdy thick-bottomed pot with a lid.

In a blender or food processor, pulverize the beer, tomatoes, anchovies, garlic, tomato paste, jalapeño, ½ bunch parsley leaves and stems, and ½ bunch cilantro leaves and stems. Since you've added stems and whole garlic cloves, make sure the mixture is puréed enough so that it's almost smooth. It won't be the prettiest color.

In a small bowl, combine the paprika, chili powder, and cinnamon.

Turn the heat on high under your pot. If you have an exhaust fan, turn it on. Open your windows. Add a tablespoon of the vegetable oil. When the oil is shimmery and smoking, add your first batch of meat. Don't slide the meat into the hot oil, because it can splash up and burn you. Use tongs. Do this in batches. It's important that you don't crowd the pieces or they will steam. Once they're searing away, there's no need to move them about. Just let them do their thing. You want them to turn a deep dark brown before flipping them over. You don't need to brown all four sides of each piece of meat. Instead, when about two sides of each piece are browned, remove from the heat and reserve on a plate. Continue with the rest of the meat. If you need to, add a splash more oil for each batch.

Turn down the heat to low. Add the olive oil to the hot pot and then the onion. Use a wooden spoon to scrape the meat goodies off the bottom of the pot. Cook for a few minutes, stirring occasionally until the onion softens. Add the dry spice mixture to the onion. Raise the heat to medium. Stir for about 30 seconds until the onion is coated and the spices have toasted a bit. Don't let them burn. Slide in the browned meat with its juices. Stir in the beer-tomato-herb mixture. Bring to a boil. Turn off the heat. Stab the lime a dozen times with a small, sharp paring knife and press it down into the stew. Cover the pot, transfer to the oven, and cook for anywhere from 2 to 4 hours. Check the stew after 2 hours.

The stew is done when the meat starts to fall apart. A nice way to test for doneness is to take out a piece and try to shred it with two forks. If the meat gives you resistance, stir the stew and return the covered pot to the oven. Continue to check every 20 minutes until the meat just falls apart. You can leave the meat in chunks or shred all of it with two forks (or your fingers when it's cool). I like it shredded because it soaks up more of the sauce. Make sure you taste it. If it's a little flat, add some salt and a splash of sherry wine vinegar. Cook for a few minutes and taste again.

If you're eating the stew that day, just place the covered pot at the back of your stovetop until dinnertime. Heat it back up before serving.

The stew will keep for a few days in the fridge. Or you can freeze it for several months.

LAMB POPSICLES

serves 4

Lamb rib chops are an indulgence, so we only eat them occasionally. We pick ours up like popsicles to make things a little less precious. I often get a rack and cut it into chops. I try to trim off some, but not all, of the excess fat along the meat and up the bone (google how to French a lamb chop with string). You can also get the butcher to do this for you. Watch them butchering so you can do it next time. It's fun.

The chops are juicy and delicious on their own. But, right after they are cooked, it's nice to squeeze lemon on them and top with chopped parsley. Or spoon some Pesto (page 195) on each cooked chop. They also work really well encircling a salad of arugula or hearts of romaine tossed with Garlic Anchovy Vinaigrette (page 201) and scattered with pomegranate arils. Honestly, almost anything goes with these as long as they're cooked properly.

1 rack of lamb cut into rib chops (usually between 6 and 8)

Kosher salt and freshly ground black pepper

1 lemon, quartered, seeds removed

Two 4-inch sprigs rosemary

4 cloves garlic, peeled

1 tablespoon extra-virgin olive oil, for the marinade

1 tablespoon vegetable oil, for cooking

Lemon wedges, for serving
Chopped parsley, for serving
Pesto (page 195), for serving

Place the chops on a sheet pan or large plate in one layer. Generously season both sides with salt and pepper.

Put the lemon, rosemary, garlic, and olive oil in a mortar. Bash with the pestle until you start to smell the rosemary and the garlic—about 20 seconds. Alternatively, you can do this by placing the marinade in a closed Ziploc bag and whacking it with the bottom of a metal bowl.

Pour the marinade over the chops, flipping them a few times until they are all coated. Let them sit for 45 minutes at room temperature. Or marinate overnight in the fridge. Just make sure to bring them to room temperature before cooking.

Crank the heat to high under a large heavy-bottomed pan (I use cast iron). Turn on your fan. Open your windows. Add the vegetable oil. Once the oil is shimmering, toss a few pieces of the garlic, lemon, and rosemary from the marinade into the pan (you won't eat them because they will burn, but they add a nice perfume to the chops). Using tongs or your hands, place the thin, fatty side of each chop into the pan. I usually lean them together (almost like reassembling the rack) just until some of the super fatty parts crisp up (about 2 minutes). Then cook for 2 minutes on each of the flat sides. The heat is high, so they will cook very quickly. You can cut into one to get the full picture. Make sure they're pink, with the rawness just disappearing from the center. Remember they will continue cooking once removed from the heat. You can always throw them back in the pan for a minute. If you want to be more precise, use an instant-read thermometer. Rare: 115° to 120°F. Medium-rare: 120° to 125°F. Medium: 130° to 135°F. Remove the chops from the pan and top with a squeeze of lemon and chopped parsley. Let them rest for 5 minutes before eating. Serve with a bowl of pesto.

HAZELNUT BUTTER COOKIES

makes 20 to 22 cookies

These are a variation on the Mexican, Russian, Swedish, or Italian tea or wedding cake: a nut cookie, dredged or sprinkled, when just out of the oven, in powdered sugar, resulting in a sweet, gooey, and lickable exterior layer.

If you can, buy unsalted pre-roasted hazelnuts. They usually have some of the skins still on, which add flavor. Or follow the instructions below to roast them yourself.

3 cups whole hazelnuts, pre-roasted, or see directions below

2 cups all-purpose flour

1 teaspoon kosher salt

1 cup unsalted butter, at room temperature

¼ cup white sugar

½ cup dark brown sugar, firmly packed

1 egg

1 tablespoon vanilla extract

1 cup powdered sugar

Preheat the oven to 350°F.

If you are toasting the hazelnuts, spread them out in a single layer on a cookie sheet and place them in the preheated oven. Roast until they're just starting to darken and smell nutty (about 10 minutes). Be careful. They will burn quickly. Remove from the oven and pour the hot nuts into a dish towel. Gather the four corners together, creating a tight package. Twist the top closed. Using your hands, press the hazelnuts into each other for about 5 minutes to remove some of the skins. Leaving most of the skins behind on the dish towel, scoop up the hazelnuts with your hands and place them in the food processor. Pulverize at full speed for 20 seconds until the pieces are about the size of peppercorns. Scoop out 1½ cups of the nuts and set aside for rolling the cookies later. Continue pulverizing until the rest of the nuts are creamy and smooth. Be patient, especially if your blade is a bit dull. It can take anywhere from 2 to 4 minutes.

Sift or whisk together the flour and salt. Set aside.

Place the butter, white sugar, brown sugar, and hazelnut butter in the bowl of a stand mixer. Beat at medium speed with the paddle attachment for 30 seconds. Scrape down the sides. Crank up to high speed and beat for another 30 seconds until fully combined with no traces of butter. Add the egg. Beat on medium speed for 10 seconds. Scrape down the sides. Add the vanilla. Beat on medium for 10 seconds. Scrape down the sides. Add the flour mixture in three batches on low speed for 10 seconds, scraping down the sides between each addition. The dough is done when there are no traces of flour left. Don't overmix. Refrigerate for at least an hour.

Line two baking sheets with Silpats or parchment paper. Spread out the reserved chopped hazelnuts on a dinner plate. Scoop out 1½-ounce balls of the chilled dough (or just eyeball about the size of a golf ball). Roll the cookies in the nuts, pressing a bit to get the pieces to stick, and place on the baking sheets. The cookies only spread a little bit, so it's fine to have them about 2 inches apart. Bake them for 15 to 18 minutes. They will just start to brown on the outside and still be quite soft inside.

Using a sifter or a fine strainer, generously sift the powdered sugar over the hot cookies. The cookies must be warm when you do this or the sugar won't stick.

Cool the cookies completely on the baking sheets. Sift some more powdered sugar over the tops before serving. They stay fresh at room temperature for up to 4 days. Or you can freeze them for up to 6 months. To bake from frozen, just turn down the oven temperature to 325°F and allow a little extra time for baking. Refresh the cookies with powdered sugar before serving.

GRANDMA'S FUDGY ICEBOX BROWNIES

makes about 40 small servings

These are adapted from a recipe my grandmother always made. The main difference is she served them right out of the oven, while I undercook them and store them in the freezer so anytime you need some brownies, they are there for you. They can be served in numerous ways—in elegant slender slices with afternoon tea, as a thick square under a scoop of ice cream for a birthday party, as the base for a baked Alaska. You can leave out both the walnuts and the chocolate chips; the cinnamon will taste more pronounced without them.

1 cup walnut halves

1½ cups unsalted butter (plus a bit more for greasing the pan; I often use the remainder on the butter paper), cubed

1½ cups all-purpose flour

¾ teaspoon cinnamon

1 teaspoon kosher salt

9 ounces unsweetened chocolate, roughly chopped

3 large eggs

2¼ cups white sugar

1 tablespoon vanilla extract

One 12-ounce bag (2 cups) of bittersweet chocolate chips

Powdered sugar, for serving

Preheat the oven to 325°F. Toast the walnuts on a cookie sheet until golden brown (8 to 10 minutes). Set aside to cool.

Butter and flour an 8-by-8-inch metal or glass cake pan.

Sift the flour, cinnamon, and salt into a bowl. Whisk to combine. Set aside.

Put the butter and chocolate in a double boiler over medium-high heat (or in a heatproof bowl placed on top of a pot of boiling water; make sure the bowl doesn't touch the water). When the butter and chocolate are almost melted (about 8 to 10 minutes), remove from the heat, and set aside to cool.

In a large bowl, whisk the eggs, sugar, and vanilla until the mixture is thick and creamy and has lightened in color—around 4 minutes by hand or 2 minutes in a stand mixer on high with a whisk attachment.

Stir the cooled butter and chocolate mixture until smooth and then slowly whisk it into the egg mixture until combined. Switch to a wooden spoon or plastic spatula. Fold in the flour mixture until there are just a few remaining pockets of flour. Fold in the walnuts and chocolate chips.

Pour the batter into the cake pan. Bake for 30 minutes. It will still be jiggly at the center. Cool completely in the pan for 3 hours. Cover with wax paper or plastic wrap and freeze in the pan, at least 6 hours or overnight.

Once frozen solid, remove from the freezer. Set the pan over a gas flame or electric cooktop, sliding it continuously for about 15 seconds (or pop in a hot oven for 1 minute). Use a paring knife to separate the brownie from the sides of the pan. Carefully invert the brick of brownies out onto a cutting board. Using a very large and sharp knife, cut the square into four 2-inch-thick rectangles. Wrap each piece in plastic wrap and store in the freezer. Pull out a brick and slice off a few brownies as needed. Serve right away, or let them soften up a bit at room temperature (about 15 minutes), and sprinkle with powdered sugar. Keep any leftover thawed brownies in an airtight container at room temperature or in the fridge for a few days.

VANILLA BEAN CUSTARD ICE CREAM

makes one generous pint

This custard-based ice cream is fabulous in between two chocolate chip cookies, on a warm cobbler, or drizzled with a dark and salty caramel sauce. But it also stands alone. Make sure to treat yourself to a large spoonful of the cooked custard before it cools.

This recipe is also a solid base for almost any ice cream you want to make. Stir ½ cup Crème Fraîche (page 189) into the custard right before you churn it. Or use half brown sugar and half white. Or, once it's churned, right before freezing, quickly stir in chocolate shavings, cookie dough, or streaks of fruit purée. Play.

I don't use anything like cream cheese or corn syrup to prevent the ice cream from getting icy in the freezer. So it's best eaten a few hours after it's made. Just enough time to firm up. Not enough time to get icy.

Warning: *Most ice cream machines require that you freeze the insert for 24 hours before churning.*

6 egg yolks
⅔ cup white sugar, divided in half
¼ teaspoon kosher salt
1½ cups half-and-half
1 vanilla bean
1½ cups heavy cream

To prepare an ice-water bath: Place a fine strainer over a medium-size bowl. Set the bottom of the medium-size bowl inside a larger bowl. Add a few handfuls of ice cubes to the larger bowl. You will add the water later.

In another medium bowl, whisk the yolks with half the sugar (⅓ cup) and salt until blended. Whisk in the half-and-half.

With a sharp paring knife, on a clean cutting board or a piece of parchment, cut the vanilla bean in half lengthwise. With the dull side of the knife, carefully scrape out the seeds.

In a medium-size heavy-bottomed saucepan (with an available lid), combine the heavy cream, the vanilla bean pods and seeds, and the remaining ⅓ cup sugar. Whisking over high heat, bring to just under a boil, stirring occasionally with a wooden spoon, then immediately turn off the heat, cover, and let steep for 5 minutes.

Slowly pour the vanilla cream mixture into the egg yolk mixture, whisking constantly. This tempers the eggs, allowing them to adjust to the change in temperature without getting stressed out and turning into scrambled eggs. If there are extra people in the kitchen, have them help you out.

Pour the custard base back into the saucepan over medium-low heat and start stirring with a wooden spoon. Don't walk away. Keep stirring. You don't want the custard to boil or bubble at all.

Watch and feel for the shift in viscosity. As you stir, the thin custard will slap against the sides of the saucepan like waves against the sides of a boat. As the custard thickens, the gliding spoon will cause it to rise up and settle back down without much of a splash. This takes anywhere from 4 to 6 minutes. But don't time it. Just watch. To confirm that it's done, do the drag-your-finger-across-the-back-of-the-wooden-spoon test. It's ready when your finger leaves a lovely lingering trail. Or if you prefer to use an instant-read thermometer, it's ready when the custard registers about 170°F.

Remove from the heat and pour the custard through the strainer into the medium-size bowl that's resting in the ice. Add enough water to the larger bowl with the ice so that the level of the water is almost to the level of the custard. If the inner bowl starts to float, it can get tippy. I've lost custard into the ice bath. So go slowly.

Leave the medium bowl in the ice bath until the custard is cool. Stir every 10 minutes or so. Refrigerate the custard for several hours or overnight.

Before churning, set a pint-size container in the freezer to chill. Churn the custard in an ice cream machine according to the manufacturer's directions. It's done when the ice cream looks like it's moving in one solid piece along with the paddle. You can also stop the machine and swipe the ice cream with your finger. If it stays put, it's done. If it's soft and caves in on itself, it needs more time. This usually takes about 20 to 25 minutes in my Cuisinart ice cream maker. Transfer the custard to the chilled container, cover, and freeze for a few hours before serving. Lick the paddle.

STRAWBERRY BALSAMIC TART

serves 6 to 8

I don't like to write recipes that require hard-to-find ingredients, but I am going to make an exception with this tart. Only make this if you can find tiny strawberries with lots of flavor. Sometimes these little baby strawberries can be found in the spring at a farmers' market. Another option is the variety called wild, Alpine, or fraises des bois.

If you have a pizza stone or a baking steel, preheat it while you assemble the tart. This tart cooks at high heat and fast, and the stone helps keep the base of the tart nice and crisp. Otherwise, a sheet pan works fine.

Warning: *If you make this tart with big and airy strawberries, there will be too much liquid and all will be a mess. So don't do it!*

- 1 recipe Tart Dough (page 181) or 1 (14-ounce) sheet puff pastry
- 3 cups small strawberries
- 1 tablespoon balsamic reduction, homemade (page 190) or store-bought (you want it syrupy, not watery)
- 1 tablespoon white sugar
- ¼ teaspoon kosher salt
- 1 tablespoon cream or half-and-half, for the crust
- 2 tablespoons turbinado sugar, for the crust

Take your tart dough out of the fridge 15 to 20 minutes ahead of time (leave out 35 to 40 minutes if it's frozen).

While the tart dough is softening, stem the strawberries and place them in a bowl. Toss them with the balsamic reduction, sugar, and salt. Leave them for 15 to 20 minutes. Stir occasionally.

Place a pizza stone or sheet pan in the oven and preheat to 400° F.

On a piece of parchment, roll out your tart dough into approximately a 13-by-4-inch rectangle, about ¼ inch thick.

Strain the berries and save the juice for later. Spread the berries down the center of the length of dough, leaving an inch clear all around the edges. Fold the long edges 1 inch into the center. The outer inch of berries will then be tucked under the border. Do the same with the short edges. Pinch the corners closed. Don't be perfect about this; it should look funky. The priority is to seal the corners up so the juice is less likely to leak when the tart is cooking.

With a pastry brush, paintbrush, or a spoon, paint any

exposed dough with the cream or half-and-half. Sprinkle the dough with the turbinado sugar.

Take your hot pizza stone or sheet pan out of the oven. Carefully slide the parchment with the tart onto the stone or pan. Bake until the crust is golden brown and the berries are soft and bubbling, about 25 to 30 minutes. A good trick is to use a spatula to try to lift up the tart. If it lifts up in one piece, it's done. If it sags, it needs a few more minutes. It might leak as it cooks. Just wipe up drips with a paper towel before they burn.

Reduce reserved juices until syrupy. This will take about a minute so don't walk away. Paint the cooked strawberries with the syrup using a pastry brush or the back of a spoon.

Serve right away with crème fraîche or ice cream. It's also good cold for breakfast.

COTTAGE CHEESE PANCAKES

makes around thirty-two 3½-inch pancakes

My parents made a version of these protein pancakes on the weekends when I was little. They got the recipe from one of our babysitters. I call them the "empty out the tubs" pancakes because I often add any creamy dairy that needs to be used up: yogurt, sour cream, cottage cheese, Crème Fraîche (page 189), quark, or ricotta. They are thin, delicate, and crêpe-like. At the same time they are quite filling. The batter is very runny, so it's essential that you pour it slowly onto the griddle from a pitcher.

We eat them with warm maple syrup, Nutella, or powdered sugar and lemon.

6 large eggs

1 cup cottage cheese

1 cup whole-milk yogurt

2 teaspoons vanilla extract

1 cup all-purpose flour

1 tablespoon white sugar

1 teaspoon baking powder

½ teaspoon kosher salt

Butter for grilling and serving (I like salted)

Place all ingredients except the butter in a blender. Blend at high speed for 20 seconds. Scrape down the sides. Blend for 10 more seconds. Pour into a pitcher. Use right away or cover and place in the fridge overnight. After a few days in the refrigerator, the batter might start to look gray or green. Don't worry. Just mix it thoroughly right before cooking and all will be well.

Crank a griddle or nonstick pan to medium-high heat. Once hot, add some butter (a few teaspoons, or just put the end of a firm stick straight down onto the grill and rub it all around). Once the butter has melted (watch that it doesn't burn), carefully pour the batter onto the griddle to form pancakes of the desired size (the batter will spatter a bit). Flip each pancake when bubbles form on the top, and the bottom is a dark caramel color (check with a spatula). They cook very fast (20 to 30 seconds per side). You'll need to keep regulating the heat between batches. Add a little more butter if needed. It's best to eat them right away. They don't hold up for long, so don't keep them warm in the oven.

Tell your partner, friend, therapist, doula, midwife, or doctor if you have feelings of depression or anxiety during breastfeeding. Ask for help if you have intrusive thoughts about harming yourself or others. Or go to the websites below. There is a lot of support out there.

Substance Abuse and Mental Health Services Administration:
    https://www.samhsa.gov (click "Find Treatment")
La Leche League International: https://www.llli.org
Postpartum Progress: https://postpartumprogress.com
Postpartum Support International: https://www.postpartum.net
Doulas of North America International: https://www.dona.org

You can e-mail me here with any questions: EverythingIsUnder
    Control2020@gmail.com

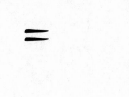

ACKNOWLEDGMENTS

Thank you to:

All the mamas who let me witness their children's births.

My grandmother Phyllis Diebenkorn, for bringing us all into the kitchen.

My grandfather Richard Diebenkorn, for showing me how to find beauty in the process, in the layers, in the chaos.

My grandmother Elizabeth Grant, for teaching me how to tell a story, how to make biscuits and peach ice cream, to always tuck a dollar bill into the bottom of my purse.

My grandfather Benjamin Grant, for his magnificent attention to language.

My mom, Gretchen Grant, for bringing us all to the table, for keeping us at the table, for defining comfort in terms of food and light.

My dad, Dick Grant, for teaching me to always take the high road, to never drink more than one martini, to always squeeze the toothpaste tube from the bottom.

My baby brother, Ben Grant, for keeping me laughing and grounded with all the chapter titles, for the ping-pong, for being proud of me.

My mother-in-law, Juli Teitelbaum, for reminding me that there is no rush, that I have time, that everything changes.

Anna Stein, for asking to be my agent before I even knew what a literary agent was, for fighting so hard for me, for always telling me the truth, for helping me kick that first lackluster book deal up, up, and away.

Emily Bell, for choosing my book, for her gentle and meticulous and beautiful editing, for telling me to stop saying I'm sorry.

Jackson Howard, for his bottomless patience, for never making me feel like an idiot.

Farrar, Straus and Giroux, for taking a risk on me and making every step feel so smooth.

Na Kim, for designing my just-messy-enough kick-ass pink cover.

Kenzi Wilbur, for reading so many versions of this book, for never letting me get away with anything, for sawing down lemon trees with me.

Emily Thelin, for recipe testing with so much love (and so many pregnancy hormones).

Nobu Matsuhisa, Michael McCarty, David Bouley, and Bill Yosses, for letting me, a hard-core beginner, revolve briefly in their extraordinary restaurant orbits.

Renee Cole Clyde, for telling me a week before she died that this book absolutely needed to be out in the world.

Erin Scott, for ten years of never-ending (phone) support.

Jeff Gordinier, for bringing so much beautiful writing into my life.

Jessica Carbone, for pushing me to write a memoir.

Stanley Love (RIP), for teaching me to dance.

Amy Cook, for always making me feel smart (even though she is the brilliant one) and for always knowing when I needed to cry, to eat, to sit down.

Marianne McCune, for walking that goat around the block in 1976 and never ever leaving my side.

And thanks to a few more cheerleaders: Kelley Kahn, Mike McCune, Marylee McCune, Claire Crawley Delgado, David Delgado, Anna Verwaal, Diane Dawson, Constance Rock, Tai Carson, Bill Isenberg, Margi Young, Michael Cecconi, Sarah Marchick, Rob Hallman, Anne Marxer, Chris Heine, Ken Weitzman, Simon Bertrang, Audra McDonald, Jen Bilik, Joanna Elliott, Jen Hofer, Trevor Carlson, Lauri Hogan, Yalda Modabber, Sarah Horwich, Laurel Leichter, Melanie Dunea, Molly Yeh, Lily Diamond, Nik Sharma, Sarah Kieffer, Carolyn Federman, Erica Tanov, Shoshana Berger, Kelly Duane, Leslie Jonath, Julia Cosgrove, Jeffery Cross, Penny Dedel, Julia Rhodes Davis, Hagar Scher, Margaret Jenkins, Johannes Sanzin, Mika, Geoffrey O'Sullivan, Reba Thomas, Geoffrey Thomas, Jen Todd, Sally Van Doren, John Van Doren, Andrea Liguori, Claire Dederer, Liz Prueitt, Jill Teitelbaum, Jorge Flores, Jennifer Durning, Morgan Oppenheimer, Samin Nosrat, Kari Stuart, Alan Ziegler, Elizabeth Minchilli, Elizabeth Gilbert, Jenny Rosenstrach, Kirk Ross, Patricia Liverman, Elissa Altman, Michael Wilson, Nikki Steen, Larry Steen, Christine Crawley, Kelly Snowden, Charlotte Druckman, Brian Bistrong.

And finally, to my kids, Bella and Dash, for being such patient, delightful, and empathetic creatures. I am never ever letting them move out of the house.

And to my husband, Matthew Ross, for saying yes when I asked him to marry me, for making me feel like a superhero, for always ordering the ragù.

A Note About the Author

Phyllis Grant is a finalist for the International Association of Culinary Professionals Award for Personal Essays / Memoir Writing and a three-time Saveur Blog Awards finalist for her blog, *Dash and Bella*. She has cooked in world-renowned restaurants, including Nobu, Michael's, and Bouley. Her essays and recipes have been published in a dozen anthologies and cookbooks, including *Best Food Writing* in both 2015 and 2016. Her work has been featured in *Esquire*, *O, The Oprah Magazine*, *The New York Times*, *Real Simple*, *Saveur*, *HuffPost*, *Time*, the *San Francisco Chronicle*, Food52, and *Salon*. She lives in Berkeley, California, with her husband and two children.